Gwen Stefani

by Anne K. Brown

LUCENT BOOKS
A part of Gale, Cengage Learning

Detroit • New York • San Francisco • New Haven, Conn • Waterville, Maine • London

LIBRARY OF CONGRESS CATALOGING-IN-PUBLICATION DATA

Brown, Anne K., 1962–
Gwen Stefani / by Anne K. Brown.
p. cm. — (People in the news)
Includes bibliographical references and index.
ISBN 978-1-4205-0126-1 (hardcover)
1. Stefani, Gwen, 1969—Juvenile literature. 2. Women singers—United States—Biography—Juvenile literature. 3. Women rock musicians—United States—Biography—Juvenile literature. I. Title.
ML3930.S74B76 2009
782.42164092—dc22
[B]

2008051289

Lucent Books
27500 Drake Rd.
Farmington Hills, MI 48331

ISBN-13: 978-1-4205-0126-1
ISBN-10: 1-4205-0126-7

Printed in the United States of America
1 2 3 4 5 6 7 13 12 11 10 09

Contents

Foreword 4

Introduction 6
Never Any Doubt

Chapter 1 9
Orange County Girl

Chapter 2 23
Not Just Luck

Chapter 3 38
A New Spark for No Doubt

Chapter 4 54
The Real Life of Gwen Stefani

Chapter 5 73
The Sound of Gwen Stefani's Music

Notes 91

Important Dates 95

For More Information 98

Index 100

Picture Credits 103

About the Author 104

Foreword

Fame and celebrity are alluring. People are drawn to those who walk in fame's spotlight, whether they are known for great accomplishments or for notorious deeds. The lives of the famous pique public interest and attract attention, perhaps because their experiences seem in some ways so different from, yet in other ways so similar to, our own.

Newspapers, magazines, and television regularly capitalize on this fascination with celebrity by running profiles of famous people. For example, television programs such as *Entertainment Tonight* devote all of their programming to stories about entertainment and entertainers. Magazines such as *People* fill their pages with stories of the private lives of famous people. Even newspapers, newsmagazines, and television news frequently delve into the lives of well-known personalities. Despite the number of articles and programs, few provide more than a superficial glimpse at their subjects.

Lucent's People in the News series offers young readers a deeper look into the lives of today's newsmakers, the influences that have shaped them, and the impact they have had in their fields of endeavor and on other people's lives. The subjects of the series hail from many disciplines and walks of life. They include authors, musicians, athletes, political leaders, entertainers, entrepreneurs, and others who have made a mark on modern life and who, in many cases, will continue to do so for years to come.

These biographies are more than factual chronicles. Each book emphasizes the contributions, accomplishments, or deeds that have brought fame or notoriety to the individual and shows how that person has influenced modern life. Authors portray their subjects in a realistic, unsentimental light. For example, Bill Gates—the cofounder and chief executive officer of the software giant Microsoft—has been instrumental in making personal computers the most vital tool of the modern age. Few dispute his business savvy, his perseverance, or his technical expertise, yet critics say he is ruthless in his dealings with competitors and driven more by his desire to maintain Microsoft's dominance in the computer industry than by an interest in furthering technology.

In these books, young readers will encounter inspiring stories about real people who achieved success despite enormous obstacles. Oprah Winfrey—the most powerful, most watched, and wealthiest woman on television today—spent the first six years of her life in the care of her grandparents while her unwed mother sought work and a better life elsewhere. Her adolescence was colored by promiscuity, pregnancy at age fourteen, rape, and sexual abuse.

Each author documents and supports his or her work with an array of primary and secondary source quotations taken from diaries, letters, speeches, and interviews. All quotes are footnoted to show readers exactly how and where biographers derive their information and provide guidance for further research. The quotations enliven the text by giving readers eyewitness views of the life and accomplishments of each person covered in the People in the News series.

In addition, each book in the series includes photographs, annotated bibliographies, timelines, and comprehensive indexes. For both the casual reader and the student researcher, the People in the News series offers insight into the lives of today's newsmakers—people who shape the way we live, work, and play in the modern age.

Never Any Doubt

"It would take an act of God for this band to get on the radio."[1] Those were the words of the program director at radio station KROQ in Los Angeles after listening to the first CD produced by the band No Doubt. He felt that the music did not fit any of the styles that were popular in 1992 and was not willing to take a risk and play it on the radio. No Doubt's dream of being heard by millions of listeners was crushed.

The band had thought that their new CD was a first step on the road to success, but what they thought was a dream coming true turned into disappointment. The CD's sales were low, and the band was not launched into fame. Yet the members of the band—Tony Kanal, Adrian Young, Tom Dumont, and Gwen Stefani—were not about to give up. They wrote new music, played concerts at small clubs, and kept their dream alive.

After releasing their third CD, the songs, the style, and the timing all fell into place for No Doubt. The new CD, called *Tragic Kingdom*, was released in October 1995. Much to No Doubt's delight, the program director at KROQ was proved wrong. Not only was their song "Just a Girl" played on the station, but it prompted huge numbers of requests. Sales of the CD eventually surpassed 10 million copies.

Those events were just a few of the highs and lows that would mark the career of No Doubt. During its ten-year career, the band enjoyed success and survived difficulties, and they persevered to sell millions of albums, become nominated for music awards, and play concerts all over the world.

At the center of the band's creative energy was a platinum blond girl in track pants and Doc Marten shoes who could pour her heart out in a ballad of lost love or pogo around the stage like a maniacal firecracker. Gwen Stefani was unlike any other singer at the time. She did not fit the mold of rocker chick or pop princess. But fans who understood her fell in love with her. Stefani brought a unique style to the music world and a unique flavor to No Doubt.

Gwen Stefani is equally well known for her solo career. She released two solo CDs and several music videos, all in her unique and colorful style. Her CDs sold millions of copies, and her music videos gathered lots of attention.

In addition to her musical talents, Stefani became recognized as a fashion icon. Onstage, at award shows, and out in public, Stefani is always dressed in an outfit that is original and in good

It took several years, but No Doubt and Gwen Stefani (left, pictured with Tony Kanal) became a huge success.

taste. She is placed on celebrity best-dressed lists and considered a fashion trendsetter. Her popularity as a musician gave her the recognition to successfully launch a line of clothing and accessories known as L.A.M.B., as well as a perfume called L.

Yet Stefani has never let her fame get the better of her. She never uses drugs or overindulges in alcohol. Her face is never splashed across gossip magazines with outrageous headlines. Although she is often photographed, she has managed to avoid the embarrassing situations that some celebrities experience.

Gwen Stefani has managed to combine a rock star lifestyle with a traditional marriage and two children. She is a wife and mom who can play at a playground or dazzle thousands of fans. Yet with so much to juggle, Stefani makes it look easy. She is surprised by her fame and success and never forgets to appreciate it. Despite her long career and millions of fans, deep down, Stefani still considers herself "just a girl."

Chapter 1

Orange County Girl

Anaheim, California, is well known as the residence of many famous and beloved personalities—Mickey and Minnie Mouse, Cinderella, Buzz Lightyear, and the entire cast of Disney characters make their homes at Disneyland, the focal point of Anaheim. The clean, friendly town in Southern California's Orange County can also lay claim as the childhood home of another popular face—Gwen Stefani. On October 3, 1969, Gwendolyn Renée was born at St. Jude Medical Center in neighboring Fullerton, California.

Gwen's parents, Dennis and Patti, welcomed their daughter home to their house less than a mile from Disneyland in Anaheim. Brother Eric was two years old when Gwen was born.

The Stefanis were an average American family for 1969. Dennis and Patti were high school sweethearts who had performed in a folk group called the Innertubes during college. When they married, they decided to settle down and raise children. Dennis became a marketing executive for Yamaha, which produced musical instruments and band equipment. Patti went to work as a dental assistant, but quit her job to stay at home when the children were born. They shared their love of music with their children, playing records of folk artists such as Bob Dylan and Emmylou Harris at home and taking the family to concerts.

Gwen was three years old when her sister Jill was born, and two years later, brother Todd joined the family. The Stefani children found many creative ways to entertain themselves. Eric enjoyed drawing

Gwen Stefani was born in Fullerton, California, on October 3, 1969. Her parents, Dennis and Patti Stefani (pictured with Gwen in 2007), shared their love of music with their children.

cartoons and playing the piano, and he often convinced Gwen to sing with him. The children held puppet shows for their friends and family. Like many girls, Gwen and Jill played house, but in their version, speaking was not allowed. The girls sang all of their conversations, and their game became known as "musical house."

Playing dress-up was also a favorite pastime. Patti Stefani taught Gwen and Jill to sew when they were very young, and they often made their own clothes, accessories, and Halloween costumes. At about the age of twelve or thirteen, Gwen developed her first fashion hobby. She liked to shop at thrift stores and then take the clothes home, take them apart, and resew them to suit her own personal style. Her bedroom turned into a tiny design workshop filled with clothes. When asked about her passion for sewing, she told *People*, "Everyone knew not to walk in my room without shoes on 'cause of the pins."[2]

The Stefani parents encouraged their children to be creative, but they also worked to raise children rooted in strong values. They were devout Catholics and taught their children to pray and attend church. The Stefanis were protective of their children and more conservative than other parents were. Eric, Gwen, Jill, and Todd were expected to observe their curfews and follow household rules. The family was structured yet close-knit, and the children felt loved and supported by their parents.

Gwen also found support and inspiration in her older brother, Eric. Whether he was cartooning, playing piano, or just hanging out with friends, Gwen felt that he was always doing something fascinating. Because he was outgoing and enjoyed attention and Gwen was quieter and more reserved, she was happy to let him try new things first and live in his shadow. Gwen trusted her brother, and he had a way of convincing her that she could do things she was afraid to try.

An Old Hollywood Wannabe

As she was growing up and in her teens, Gwen loved watching movies. Old Hollywood films and glamour became a fascination for her. She loved watching black-and-white movies starring Jean Harlow, Marilyn Monroe, and Sophia Loren. Her bedroom was covered in pictures of Marilyn Monroe. She loved the elegant dresses, elaborate rhinestones, and graceful styles of the movie wardrobes from the 1930s and 1940s, especially the flowing lines, figure-hugging skinny silhouettes, and upswept hair. The looks were conservative, yet feminine, and they would inspire her fashion tastes over and over again.

Her love of Old Hollywood would later provide Gwen with inspiration for her high school prom dress. Gwen made her own dress, copying a gown worn by actress Grace Kelly in Alfred Hitchcock's movie *Rear Window*.

Gwen Stefani has drawn some of her fashion looks from Old Hollywood stars such as Jean Harlow, whom she played in the movie The Aviator.

An Unlikely Idol

Gwen loved many movies, including the musical *Annie*, but one of the most captivating for her was *The Sound of Music*. A romantic musical, it tells the story of an Austrian naval captain who falls in love with the governess he hires to watch over his seven children. One of the most popular films of its time, Gwen considers it her favorite movie.

Gwen became a fan of Julie Andrews, who played the troubled Maria, and identified with her character. In the movie, Maria makes her own clothes, and she even makes play clothes for all

The Sound of Music

In 1965 *The Sound of Music* appeared in movie theaters across the United States, and it became an instant classic. Audiences loved the story of Maria, a young woman aspiring to become a nun at a convent in Austria. Mother Abbess, believing that Maria has another calling, sends her to serve as a governess for seven children. Maria quickly wins over the family and unexpectedly falls in love with their father, a retired captain in the Austrian navy. Shortly after they marry, their family must escape Austria to avoid the Nazi influence that is infiltrating their homeland.

The movie is filled with memorable music by Richard Rodgers and Oscar Hammerstein, such as "Sixteen Going on Seventeen," "My Favorite Things," "I Have Confidence," and "The Sound of Music." The movie won five Academy Awards, including best picture, best director, and best music. Julie Andrews, in the role of Maria, was nominated for best actress.

As Gwen Stefani's favorite movie, *The Sound of Music* has influenced her throughout her life. In her music video for "Wind It Up," Gwen imitates scenes and costumes from the film and borrows music and yodeling from the song "The Lonely Goatherd."

seven children using the fabric from old draperies. "I feel like there are similarities between me and Maria," Gwen admits. "We both like to sing and sew."[3]

Teenage Gwen

The Stefani children attended Loara High School in Anaheim. Feeling she needed to lose weight, Gwen joined the swim team and swam well enough to earn the nickname "Frog." She joined the marching band as a piccolo player. Her cheerful and outgoing personality during high school also earned her the nickname "Sunshine."

Members of No Doubt, Adrian Young (left), Gwen Stefani, and Tony Kanal, swim before a beach concert in Newport Beach, California, in July 1989. A stong swimmer, Gwen had earned the nickname "Frog" while on her high school swim team.

Gwen's conservative upbringing influenced her teen years. She never had a boyfriend and did not have a large group of friends, but she did have one very close and important girlfriend. Although she took school seriously, Gwen struggled with her grades and worried that she might not get into college. She would often daydream in class about getting married or draw pictures in her notebooks.

Like many kids, Gwen was very attached to the family dog—a small, blond-colored Lhasa Apso named Marilyn, after Marilyn Monroe. Gwen eventually started calling the dog "Lamb," since it followed her everywhere, as in the nursery rhyme "Mary Had a Little Lamb."

While in high school, Gwen started her first job. She took a position at a Dairy Queen restaurant, where her work included a lot of cleaning. She and her fellow employees spent a lot of time eating when managers were not around. That experience taught her that she would always have to watch her eating habits or risk gaining a lot of weight.

Gwen remained well liked and confident in high school, yet she stood out from her fellow students. She did not enjoy the same styles or music as other teens. Her wardrobe had a heavy tomboy influence, with jeans and track suits, and she favored a brand of shoes known as Doc Martens. The footwear was a clunky brand of shoe favored by punk rockers and goth kids. Yet Gwen did not abandon femininity. Makeup was important to her, and she blended girlish makeup with her boyish styles. This mixture of tomboy and girlishness would become a trademark style for her.

The Discovery of Ska

Gwen enjoyed the dance music of the 1980s, but her favorite style of music was ska, a cross between reggae and punk. Both Gwen and her brother Eric became hooked on ska when they discovered a song called "Baggy Trousers" by a British band called Madness. Gwen began following ska music and dressing in the punky style of British ska. For a time, she wore only black-and-white clothes and hoop earrings.

The Ska Music Style

Ska music got its start in Jamaica in the late 1950s. It has a distinctive sound that uses guitar, bass, piano, drums, and horns, especially saxophone, trumpet, and trombone. The rhythms of ska are designed for dancing and are what many people associate with the Caribbean flavor of music. Ska was enjoyed by many people and spread throughout the world.

The ska movement faded in the late 1960s, but it saw a revival in England in the 1970s. Musical groups blended ska with punk rock music that was popular at the time, and the new style became known as two-tone ska. Groups such as Madness, The Selecter, and The Specials were at the forefront of the new ska scene, and these groups caught the attention of Eric and Gwen Stefani.

Two-tone ska also faded, but in the 1990s, another revival came along. Third-wave ska drew heavily from two-tone ska, and it can be heard in the music of bands such as Fishbone, The Toasters, Reel Big Fish, and No Doubt.

Gwen and Eric searched out other ska music and looked for local ska bands. A passionate piano player, Eric experimented with the ska style. Gwen recalled that she would often wake up in the morning to the sound of Eric banging away on the piano.

A Push into Music

Although Gwen enjoyed singing just for fun, she had never felt a desire to sing in public. Eric, on the other hand, thought about joining a band, and he experimented with writing songs. He convinced Gwen to sing his first song, "Stick It in the Hole," which was about a pencil sharpener. Eric had always encouraged Gwen to sing with him when they were little, and in high school he again pushed her to sing.

Because of Eric's encouragement, Gwen soon discovered that she had a good singing voice. He convinced her to take part in a

Gwen Stefani has always been close to her brother Eric. They sang together as children, and both were in the band No Doubt.

high school talent show, and she sang a song called "On My Radio" by a ska band called The Selecter.

Gwen flaunted her own personal style and her love of *The Sound of Music* for that event. She and her mother duplicated one of Maria's dresses from the movie—a fitted tweed dress with a short cape that Maria wore the first time she met the children she was to care for. In the movie, one of the children described the outfit as the ugliest dress she had ever seen, but Gwen was completely in love with it.

"The first time I ever went on stage, at a high school talent show—the dress I wore was the dress that Maria wears when she sings 'I Have Confidence.' The drop-tweed dress. I had that dress. I made it,"[4] she remembered fondly. As much as Gwen loved sewing, she was on the verge of discovering that she had another great talent waiting to be tapped.

Beginnings of a Band

As Gwen was finishing her sophomore year of high school in 1985, Eric graduated from Loara High. He began forming a band with friend John Spence, whom he had met working at Dairy Queen. Both of them were huge fans of ska, funk, and punk music. Eric had been impressed by his sister's singing ability in the talent show, and he asked her to join his band as a backup singer. Gwen was reluctant to sing in a band but agreed to try it. The threesome considered calling their band Apple Core, but eventually settled on No Doubt, one of John's favorite phrases.

No Doubt had been born. The band heavily favored the ska sound but did not try to copy other ska bands. No Doubt incorporated rock, reggae, punk, and any other styles that suited them. During the summer of 1986, Eric and John recruited six other musicians, including saxophone and trumpet players.

John Spence served as the group's lead singer, and true to the punk style, he screamed out lyrics more often than he sang them. His trademark was a fuzzy hat that he called his "fuzzy furry." And he drew screams from fans by doing backflips onstage.

Rounding out the band were Eric on keyboards, Alan Meade and Gabriel Gonzalez on trumpet, Tony Meade on saxophone,

Jerry McMahon on guitar, Chris Leal on bass, and Chris Webb as drummer. Gwen sang backup and shared vocals with John. They played for the first time at a party on December 31, 1986. Over the next few months, they played at more parties while they looked for a chance to play at a club or local concert.

First Step into Stardom

The band's first major appearance came at Fenders Ballroom in Long Beach, California, on March 12, 1987. No Doubt appeared second in a lineup of fourteen bands, with a group called The Untouchables as the main act. That night, a musician named Tony Kanal was in the audience. Tony was drawn in by the sound and style of No Doubt, and within a few weeks learned that the band was looking for a new bass player to step in for Chris Leal. Tony auditioned for the band and was invited to join. Within a few

Gwen Stefani and Tony Kanal perform with No Doubt during the halftime show of Super Bowl XXXVII. The two were a couple in the early days of the band.

months, he was recognized for his organizational talents and also became the band's unofficial manager.

While Tony was settling into his new roles with No Doubt, Gwen was finishing her senior year of high school. She graduated from Loara High in the spring of 1987. Her deepest secret at the time was that she had developed a crush on Tony, and she waited for the right moment to reveal her feelings.

In the summer of 1987, after playing at a party, Gwen asked Tony to go for a walk. She kissed him, but Tony told Gwen it would not work for them to date since they were in the band together. Gwen could not take *no* for an answer—she was in love

Gwen Stefani sings in a concert at The Roxy, in Hollywood, California, in September 1989, about a year after becoming lead singer of the band following Alan Meade's departure.

with him. Soon Tony admitted that he had feelings for Gwen. They agreed to date but swore to keep it a secret.

Gwen's life became busy and hectic during the summer and fall of 1987. The band was working hard to write music, practice, and look for chances to perform. Gwen enrolled at California State University at Fullerton to study art. In addition, she worked a job at the makeup counter at the Anaheim Plaza Mall. And she continued to date Tony in secret.

As the months passed, No Doubt received one of its biggest breaks. The band was invited to play at The Roxy, a famous club on Hollywood's Sunset Strip. For more than fifty years, the Sunset Strip had been a Hollywood hot spot filled with rock and comedy clubs, restaurants, boutiques, nightclubs, and celebrities. The Strip was made famous in movies and television shows. Gwen and the band knew that a performance at The Roxy could get them noticed by new fans—as well as record executives who sought out new talent. It would be the chance of their lifetimes.

Bouncing Back from Tragedy

John Spence pushed the group to practice every day and to polish their act. As their December performance drew near, the group looked forward to their big opportunity, but they also felt tremendous pressure to do their best. Then a tragic and unexpected event happened.

On December 21, 1987, the band learned that John Spence had taken a gun to an Anaheim park and committed suicide. He left a two-page letter explaining that he was unhappy. He felt terrible pressure about the band. But none of his friends suspected that John was in such anguish. All of them were devastated, and Eric in particular wished he could have done something to save his friend.

At first, the band decided to quit. They had lost their lead singer and did not want to continue without their friend. Yet they knew that John would want them to keep playing. The band members pulled themselves together and put on their performance at The Roxy. During the performance, they announced that it would be their last concert.

No Doubt dissolved as they grieved for John. As the days passed, they gradually realized that he would have wanted them to stay together and continue their music. They decided to try again and keep No Doubt alive, and they chose Alan Meade to take over the lead vocals.

John's death reminded his friends of the importance of loved ones. It inspired Gwen and Tony to stop hiding their romance, and they announced to the rest of the group that they were seeing each other. Eric and the others were worried at first that the relationship would harm the group, but eventually they all came to see that it was the right thing for Gwen and Tony. All of them accepted the romance, and it became just another facet of the band's makeup.

The spring of 1988 brought a new face to No Doubt. Jerry McMahon said farewell to the band, and Tom Dumont joined the group as its new guitar player. Tom had previously played in a heavy metal band but had grown tired of the out-of-control fans associated with heavy metal and wanted to play concerts that were more about the music. Tom was impressed by No Doubt's sound and quickly adapted to its style.

Alan Meade had taken over the band's vocals but quit after less than a year to take care of his pregnant girlfriend. Eric Stefani felt that Gwen was the best choice to step in as lead singer. The idea terrified Gwen, but because she trusted her brother, she agreed to try singing up front instead of in the background.

Throughout 1987 and 1988, the band began to develop a following. They played more concerts, in particular as opening acts for the punk/ska/funk band Fishbone and the punk band The Untouchables. No Doubt also recorded demo tapes, and fans eagerly purchased them at their shows. The band had struggled through some hard times, but with their newfound acceptance by more fans, everyone was willing to work hard and see where No Doubt might eventually end up.

Chapter 2

Not Just Luck

Rock bands are sometimes like recipes—they need the right combination of ingredients, flavors, and cooking time to turn out perfectly. If No Doubt was a recipe, then it was still looking for the right ingredients in 1989.

In that year saxophonist Tony Meade and drummer Chris Webb left the group. Adrian Young, a huge fan of No Doubt, auditioned to be its new drummer. Young told the group he had played in a band for seven years, even though he had been in a band for only a year and had owned his own drum kit for only two years. The group members were impressed with his talents, and Young became the band's new drummer. Young brought a free spirit and wild influence to No Doubt.

The changes in band members brought new styles and flavors to No Doubt, sometimes without the band even realizing it. Instead of playing purely ska music, their sound began to take on a distinctive and unique style. As the group wrote songs together, each member brought something new to their ska roots—a little heavy metal, a little funk, a little pop.

Tom Dumont unintentionally brought his own spin to No Doubt. He explained:

> I didn't really have a deep knowledge of the ska scene. I tried to fit in quickly, but I never seriously studied the ska idiom. I never, for example, sat down with a Madness record and tried to learn the guitar riffs. I kind of picked up the general

Julie Andrews

One of Gwen Stefani's favorite actresses, Julie Andrews, became famous for her many movie musical appearances. She is best known for her role as the "practically perfect" Mary Poppins in the movie *Mary Poppins* (for which she won the Academy Award for best actress). Her equally popular role is that of the outspoken and kindhearted Maria in *The Sound of Music.*

Recently, Andrews has had a run of royal movie parts. She played Queen Clarisse Rinaldi in *The Princess Diaries* and *The Princess Diaries 2: Royal Engagement.* She also served as the voice of Queen Lillian in *Shrek 2* and *Shrek the Third* and was the narrator in the movie *Enchanted.*

Andrews has received a number of awards. Most notably, Queen Elizabeth II made her a Dame Commander of the British Empire in 2000. This title is the female equivalent of the men's honor of being dubbed a knight.

Dame Andrews bounced back from adversity in 1997 when an operation on her throat left her unable to sing. After years of recovery, she regained the use of her voice and sang a song called "Your Crowning Glory" in the movie *The Princess Diaries 2: Royal Engagement.*

> gist of things from the other guys in the band. It turned out to be a blessing in disguise, because we ended up sounding unlike any other ska band.[5]

Tony Kanal also sensed the shift in the band's flavor. Each member was influenced by different music, including Jimi Hendrix, Steely Dan, Journey, KISS, Black Sabbath, and Prince—and for Gwen, *The Sound of Music*, as well as the ska band Madness, Julie Andrews, Kermit the Frog, and Fishbone's Angelo Moore. Kanal knew that despite their diverse musical tastes, it felt right at the time. "I guess when you take all that, we're bound to produce an open-ended sound. None of us would want it any other way. You know, just one sound would be so limited and boring."[6]

Gwen, too, could feel the band evolving into something unique. She says: "I look at our band as kinda like The Police. They had the reggae/ska thing happening, but they're a rock band. Our roots are ska, but ska just bubbles under in our music. We don't label our sound by that term."[7]

Just a Girl

One of Gwen's biggest challenges in working with the band at that time was the simple fact that she was a girl. Gwen had to overcome the attitudes of fans and the music industry. Very few women were performing in ska, punk, or reggae bands at the time. And the ones who were sported a distinctive rocker appearance—dark hair and eyeliner, leather clothes, and hard-core styles. Gwen's platinum blond hair, red lipstick, and movie-queen makeup was far outside the rock band norm.

Gwen explains: "Whenever we went to a club, I would always be looked upon as a tagalong girlfriend. [They would ask,] 'Where's your wristband?' But as soon as I finished a show, the same people

Adrian Young, Gwen Stefani, Tony Kanal, and Tom Dumont all brought their own unique flavor to No Doubt, and the band's popularity continued to grow as a result.

Gwen Stefani's *Bindi*

For a period of time around 1995 and 1996, Gwen Stefani made a fashion statement by wearing a *bindi*. A custom among women in India, a *bindi* is a dot of red makeup worn between the eyebrows, just above the bridge of the nose. Stefani discovered the custom while dating Tony Kanal, whose parents were from East India. Kanal's mother wore a *bindi* according to her home custom.

Stefani favored a *bindi* that resembled a jewel, and sometimes wore a double jewel, with a larger stone placed above a smaller one. Her use of the *bindi* caused a major stir among fashion and music industry publications.

would be like, 'Ooh, I can't believe you were up there!'"[8] Gwen remembered that she was even given rude stares by the girls in the audience, as if she did not belong onstage with the band.

Chasing Success

Throughout 1989 and 1990 No Doubt played more concerts than ever and saw a huge increase in its fans. The band gained popularity with college crowds after it began opening for bands such as Red Hot Chili Peppers, Mano Negro, and Ziggy Marley. The mailing list that Tony Kanal had started in 1987 with a few hundred names grew to include more than two thousand fans. Nonetheless, Gabriel Gonzales departed from the band in 1990, making No Doubt a five-member group—Eric, Gwen, Tony, Adrian, and Tom.

With their fan base on the rise, the group expected to catch the interest of a record company before long. No Doubt had evolved into a group with a unique sound, and they thought that surely their original musical style deserved a CD. As it turned out, the group's style actually turned away the record companies. Music executives did not understand No Doubt. They had never heard

Gwen Stefani was not the typical lead singer of a '90s rock band, but her uniqueness helped make No Doubt popular.

the band's unique sound before and did not know how to classify it—as rock, pop, punk, or any other style. They were reluctant to produce a CD with the group because they did not know how to sell it. Record companies told No Doubt that they needed to sound more like a specific current style and that their songs needed to sound more similar. The group decided to ignore that advice and stay true to themselves.

Eventually, No Doubt caught the eye of Tony Ferguson, who worked for Interscope Records. Ferguson had mixed feelings about the band. With grunge music in style, he thought it would be difficult to sell the band, with its unusual style, horn section, and a blond female lead singer who looked nothing like a punk, grunge, or rock performer. But he was impressed that the band was selling out its small shows. Ferguson pushed Jimmy Iovine, the head of Interscope, to attend a concert and consider producing No Doubt's CD. Iovine liked what he saw. No Doubt signed its first contract with Interscope Records to produce a CD in 1991. Iovine predicted that Gwen would be a star in five years.

Big Break, Hard Work

After signing the record contract, it would have been easy for No Doubt to think they had found success. They dreamed of hearing their music played on radio station KROQ, one of the biggest stations in Los Angeles and a major influence on radio stations across the country. But the group realized they had a long way to go. All of them kept their jobs in order to support themselves. Tony Kanal and Gwen continued working at a department store, Tom Dumont ran a small business renting music equipment, and Adrian Young worked as a waiter in a steak house. Eric had taken a job working as a layout artist for the animated series *The Simpsons*.

From October to December in 1991, No Doubt was constantly juggling schedules. Gwen was in art school, Tom was studying music at a community college, and Tony and Adrian were psychology majors. Amid their school and work schedules, they had to squeeze in time to record the fourteen tracks that would appear on their CD. This required making many trips to recording studios in Los Angeles—a drive of thirty to ninety minutes each way depending on traffic.

Gwen Stefani and No Doubt perform at a Christmas concert sponsored by Los Angeles rock station KROQ in December 2001. Nine years earlier, the station had refused to play their music.

They soon found that the process of making the CD was not easy. Interscope provided little support for recording and marketing the CD. The band did most of the work of recording and promoting the CD on their own. They set up their own Web site, created their own T-shirts and merchandise, and produced flyers for their mailing list. Tony Ferguson recalled that the band did a remarkable job of marketing their CD, with Kanal organizing the group and managing their business matters.

No Doubt's first CD, titled *No Doubt*, was released in March 1992. The CD was barely noticed by fans and radio stations as a result of heavy competition from grunge bands such as Pearl Jam and Nirvana, which had the hottest music in Los Angeles at the time. Grunge was selling records; alternative sounds like No Doubt went ignored.

Eric Stefani

In the 1980s Eric Stefani discovered a record by a band called Madness that would forever change his life. Hooked on the song "Baggy Trousers," Stefani played the record constantly. He attempted to learn the style and used to wake up his sister by pounding on the piano. In 1986 Stefani discovered that his friend John Spence shared his musical tastes. The pair struck upon the idea to start a band, and they invited a reluctant Gwen Stefani to join.

The band developed into No Doubt, which struggled for many years but eventually made music history with its CD sales and concert tours. Eric Stefani was the band's first keyboard player and wrote many of No Doubt's early songs. He is credited by the rest of the band as a perfectionist who always drove them to improve and be more creative.

In 1994 Stefani left No Doubt to pursue a different career. He took a full-time job as an animator on the hit TV series *The Simpsons*. Stefani lives in the Los Angeles area, not far from the rest of his family.

No Doubt sold thirty thousand copies. Interscope Records considered the CD a terrible failure compared to other albums that were selling five hundred thousand copies and becoming certified gold records. Radio station KROQ refused to play No Doubt's music. The band's biggest accomplishment—their first CD—turned into a disappointment.

No Doubt would not give up. Interscope provided money for them to go on tour, so they piled themselves into two vans, along with five other musicians and crew and all of their equipment, and set out on tour. They played thirteen shows in two weeks in the western United States. After returning home briefly, the band embarked on a second two-week tour over the summer.

"Trapped in a Box"

In 1992 music videos had been around for just over ten years. The music industry had discovered the value in producing a music video—it exposed new songs to millions of viewers and potential customers. A music video on a channel such as MTV might launch a new band toward huge record sales.

Interscope also understood the value of appearances on MTV and budgeted a mere five thousand dollars for No Doubt to produce a video. In between their tours the band filmed a video for the song "Trapped in a Box." The song, based on a poem written by Tom Dumont, describes Tom's feelings about television. He hated being sucked into a TV program and feeling like a zombie after watching it. The finished song was a collaboration of the entire band and showed a distinctive punk influence.

The music video features Gwen belting out vocals. Scenes of the band alternate between a tiny, cramped room and a spacious studio. The band members stare glassy-eyed at a television, and fans gaze zombie-like at No Doubt performing on TV. Some scenes show the band playing on the roof of their house—in those shots, they are carefree and uninhibited while away from the television. The video also shows the beginnings of a habit adopted by drummer Adrian Young—in most scenes, he is wearing only boxer shorts and his socks and boots.

Music video channel MTV took no interest in the video and never played it. Had the video been played on MTV, it might have given No Doubt exposure to a new audience and garnered thousands of fans.

Life on the Rocky Road

With tour money still available from Interscope, the time had come to reach new fans and stretch beyond the West Coast. In the fall of 1992 No Doubt embarked on its third and longest tour. They piled into two vans and traveled across the United States for two and a half months. They played at small clubs and performed as the opening act for bands such as Public Enemy and The Special Beat.

The tour had highs and lows. Some nights, No Doubt played for big crowds of up to one thousand people who enjoyed their music. Other nights, audiences were small and hostile. As the opening act for other bands, No Doubt sometimes played for crowds that had come for completely different music. But the tour gave the group experience and helped them to bond as a band and a family.

After returning from the tour, the band had to decide upon its next move. They began writing new songs and recording for their next album. With their first album launched, they expected that Interscope would back a second album and that the band was well on its way to fame.

Getting work done on songs for the second album was streamlined by the convenience of No Doubt having a home base. Eric Stefani and a friend, Eric Keyes, lived in a house on Beacon Street in Anaheim, and it became a hub of songwriting and rehearsing. The members of No Doubt came and went as their work demanded. The garage was eventually transformed into a recording studio.

Tensions with Interscope

Interscope was disillusioned by the low sales of *No Doubt* and was not enthusiastic about producing another CD. The band pitched song after song to the company, but was repeatedly told to try

No Doubt took its first long tour in the fall of 1992. They were an opening act for two and a half months.

again. Interscope gave the band a new producer named Matthew Wilder, and the band was both frustrated and annoyed by repeated requests to change their music to match the current styles and trends.

Gwen and the band spent the next three years in a tug-of-war with Interscope. Tony Kanal summarized the situation: "One of the reasons this record took so long to come out is that we withstood a lot of pressures and we were unwilling to compromise on a lot of things."[9]

"It was a really hard time. We were working, writing, attending school, trying to use up time," Gwen explained. "But every day, we were calling up [Interscope] and going, 'When can we go in? When? When? When?'"[10]

Farewell, Eric

The tough days of the early 1990s got even tougher in 1994. Eric Stefani had been working with the band as always, writing songs for the next CD, rehearsing, and recording. The band was on its way to finishing its next CD. But Eric decided that his heart was in a different place. He made the difficult decision to tell his sister and the band that he wanted to quit. He planned to follow another dream—working full-time as an animator for the TV series *The Simpsons*.

Gwen was crushed. She had idolized Eric ever since they were little. The departure put stress on their relationship as brother and sister. At the urging of their parents, Gwen and Eric went into therapy to repair their family bond. After several months, they worked though their differences and restored the closeness that they had always shared.

The rest of the band felt lost without Eric. He had driven the band to write songs and to learn to make their songs better. Gwen recalled that Eric focused on every detail. At Eric's direction, the band would work hard on the smallest things until they got them right. Sometimes he would stay up late at night and rewrite sections of a song or develop new musical elements. The other band members were worried that without Eric's influence, they might not survive.

A Crushing Split

Eric's departure from the group was difficult for Gwen. Then things turned even worse. She had been dating Tony Kanal for about seven years and felt certain that they would marry. She had never had other serious boyfriends and considered him the love of her life. They had struggled in their relationship for a few years, since they spent so much time together in the band and worked in the same department store. Stefani felt very dependent on Kanal, but he was feeling too much pressure. He told her that he wanted to break off their relationship.

Tom Dumont and Adrian Young also had to deal with the crisis of the breakup. Some bands might have completely collapsed under the circumstances. Stefani and Kanal worked hard not to let their split affect the band. Dumont gave his thoughts: "People have to follow their own hearts. I think they still care deeply for each other but it's hard to break up with your girlfriend and then live with her [on tours]. That's a tall order. They've done a great job of pulling it off. When we're all together, we get along pretty good."[11]

Stefani was devastated, but she knew she could not give up on life. She began writing more songs as a way of dealing with her feelings. She and Kanal both had the band, which they loved, to keep them busy and help them move forward. They managed to remain friends even after splitting. Stefani shared her theories about the event in *Cosmopolitan*:

> I think it was probably the passion for music. We just loved the band so much, and I guess we knew that it was worth it. But him breaking up with me was the most incredible thing, because before that, I was a very passive person who was dependent on him for my happiness. I was only seventeen when I started seeing him, and I never had any other serious boyfriends before that, so I glamorized the relationship and I was so in love. When he broke up with me, I started writing all these songs, and I found my talent, which was the most empowering thing that has ever happened to me.[12]

Gwen Stefani and Tony Kanal broke up in 1994 but remain friends and bandmates to this day.

Stefani's pain turned into hidden treasure for No Doubt. Her feelings about the breakup and picking up the pieces turned into several songs for the next album, including "End It on This," "Hey You," "Happy Now?" "Sunday Morning," "Spiderwebs," and "Don't Speak." With Gwen's new material, the group turned back to its shared goal of completing their next CD.

Tired of Waiting

After having so much trouble with Interscope, the band nearly gave up on their contract. Nearly three years had passed since the release of *No Doubt*, and they still had not finished their second CD.

Over the course of a long weekend in early 1995, the group got busy and recorded ten songs on their own in the garage on Beacon Street and turned out an entire full-length CD. The band cut one thousand copies of the new CD that they titled *The Beacon Street Collection*. For the cover of the album, they chose a photo of Gwen and Eric's grandfather doing a trick with his pet parakeet—the bird was perched on his lower lip, leaning way into his open mouth. They sold out of all the CDs at local concerts and record stores.

Chapter 3

A New Spark for No Doubt

Hoping to motivate Interscope to release their next CD, No Doubt showed *The Beacon Street Collection* to the producers at the record company, who were amazed at the work the band had done. Tony Ferguson and others were inspired to get the band busy on their next album. After years of sporadic recording in eleven different studios, the fourteen tracks were finally finished after a few more months.

Ferguson took the recordings to a colleague named Paul Palmer to get his opinion of the record. Palmer was the head of Trauma Records, one of Interscope's partners. Trauma was also working with a grunge band called Bush. Palmer was impressed with No Doubt's tracks. He says: "I thought they were fantastic the minute I heard the music. I had a feeling about the band I couldn't let go of."[13] Palmer took over the completion of the CD, finishing up the mixing and then polishing it to be ready for the final release. No Doubt felt lucky finally to have the CD under the wing of someone who understood their music.

Interscope was still nervous, as explained by Ferguson: "There were always questions about what we were going to do with this band, because rock was in this alternative grunge thing. Here we had this ska-influenced, pop-ish, hook-driven band with a blond girl singer."[14] Interscope was also concerned about Stefani's off-beat fashions—they did not understand her tomboyish clothes and clunky shoes paired with glamorous hair and makeup that looked like a movie queen from the 1940s. She looked nothing like any other female rocker at the time.

Even Stefani questioned where she fit in with other female rockers. With grunge music at its peak, many singers had a style that was loud, angry, and bitter. "All the women around me that I could look at were . . . angry, and I didn't really feel like that," she says. "And the other ones were these folky girls, so there wasn't really anybody until I discovered Blondie. She was sexy and she wasn't ashamed to be rocking out, and to me, that's having it all."[15]

Ready for Takeoff

Trauma Records and its parent, Interscope, were ready to launch the record in spite of their concerns. Prior to the release, they signed No Doubt to the Warped Tour, in which No Doubt traveled with other alternative rock bands to stadiums across the country. The bands performed along with extreme sports exhibitions, such as skateboarding and BMX biking. No Doubt traveled during August and September 1995. The new CD, titled *Tragic Kingdom*, was released in October 1995.

The CD got off to a slow start. Once again, radio station KROQ was not interested in playing the band's music. Fans were paying attention, though, and the record's sales began to climb. The song "Just a Girl" was quickly becoming a favorite at concerts, and Stefani encouraged the girls in the audience to scream out "I'm a girl!"—often with swear words in the sentence.

Stefani's swearing got her into some trouble with her mother, even though she was twenty-six years old at the time. No Doubt was preparing for a concert at a Virgin Records Megastore in the Los Angeles area. Patti Stefani had invited relatives to watch the show, and she asked her daughter not to swear during the performance. The request annoyed Gwen, and she cursed anyway. Patti Stefani would not speak to her daughter for a full week after the concert. Gwen, who had always been close to her mother, was devastated that her mom was so angry and had to apologize for her swearing and patch things up.

"Just a Girl" was helping the band to gain popularity, and over the winter of 1995, an old dream was realized for No Doubt. Radio station KROQ played "Just a Girl"—and kept on playing it. The station received a huge number of requests for the song. In

No Doubt was part of the Warped Tour in 1995, and the band traveled across the country with other alternative rock bands. Their song "Just a Girl" was gaining popularity and reached number 10 on the singles chart.

January 1996 *Tragic Kingdom* sold enough copies to land on *Billboard* magazine's Top 200 chart, debuting at number 175. The single "Just a Girl" reached the number 10 spot on the singles chart, and the video was played regularly on MTV.

Early 1996 delivered more milestones for No Doubt. The band played on *Late Night with Conan O'Brien* in January and on the *Late Show with David Letterman* in March.

New Tour, New Chances, New Milestones

May brought the beginning of a long tour for No Doubt. Paul Palmer arranged for the group to travel as the opening act for the British grunge band Bush. The tour comprised sixty shows and lasted several months. Stefani brought incredible energy to No Doubt's shows and became known for her pogo-style hopping, karate kicking, running, and dancing all over the stage. She even climbed the speakers, which her producers discouraged. Stefani slowed down only after she broke her foot during a concert and could no longer perform some of her moves.

Working with Bush was a pivotal time in Stefani's life. Gavin Rossdale, lead singer for Bush, became interested in Stefani from the moment he met her. Stefani, on the other hand, was not interested in him. She let him know that she was not looking to date anyone—especially a rock star. Rossdale persisted, and she eventually agreed to go out with him.

Her bandmates did not approve of the relationship. No Doubt was beginning to realize its dreams—the CDs, bigger tours, more fame. Stefani and Kanal had broken up about two years earlier, and Stefani had never quite recovered. Her life had been romantically sheltered until that point. And her band brothers felt that they simply could not trust a rock star like Rossdale. But Stefani began to like Rossdale more and more, and they began to see each other steadily.

As the summer tour with Bush continued, No Doubt received good news. On June 26, 1996, *Tragic Kingdom* was awarded a gold record for selling five hundred thousand copies. That same month,

In 1996 No Doubt toured as the opening act for the British band Bush. Shortly after, Gwen Stefani began dating Bush's lead singer, Gavin Rossdale.

"Spiderwebs" reached the number five spot on the *Billboard* magazine charts. And in August *Tragic Kingdom* was certified both platinum and multiplatinum. The band had taken giant steps beyond the meager thirty-thousand-copy sales of *No Doubt*.

Across the Pond—and Beyond

No Doubt's tour took them around the world beginning in June 1996. The band performed in Europe, Australia, New Zealand, Indonesia, Japan, and other countries.

The visit to Japan provided a life-changing experience for Stefani. She discovered the Harajuku shopping district of Tokyo, an area where teenage girls dressed in the most extreme fashion styles they could imagine. The fashions bordered on costumes, and Stefani became permanently fascinated by the outrageous styles and trends. Already becoming a fashion icon at that time, her exposure to Harajuku permeated her tastes from then on.

The world tour brought popularity and media attention to No Doubt. Yet some of the publicity brought a new stress to the band.

Pushed into the Spotlight

Even though No Doubt was a band and not the backup group for a solo act, the media focused its attention on Stefani. Likewise, teenage girls began copying Stefani's unique style and soon became

As a result of Stefani's unique style, the media began focusing most of its attention on her, rather than No Doubt as a whole. This caused tension with the rest of the band.

known as "Gwenabees." In writing an article for *US* magazine, Kim France attempted to explain it:

> Part of it is that she's just so cute. Then there's her vampish, playful performance style: One moment she's stalking across the stage like a rapper; the next, she's furiously pogoing. But most compelling is her truly unique sense of style. With the platinum '40s hairdo, the Indian jewel between her eyes, the constantly bare midriff, and the Southern California skateboard gear, Stefani is part Barbie doll, part club kid, and part Hindu goddess.[16]

Even the music industry press focused on Stefani, seeming to forget all about the rest of the band. Dumont, Kanal, and Young tried not to let it bother them, but being largely ignored caused tension. They were diplomatic about it in public, but they were not afraid to point out that the band was made up of four people, not just one. Yet they all understood why the media would set their sights on Stefani and forget the others. She was cute, blond, a woman, had unmatched fashion sense, and was a maniac onstage.

"Don't Speak"

The popularity of the song "Don't Speak" turned more focus on Stefani and caused new tension in the band. The song shot to number one on *Billboard* magazine's Hot 100 Airplay chart in November 1996. A heart-wrenching ballad about the breakup of a relationship, Stefani's agonized vocals drew attention like never before. Interviewers lined up to talk to Stefani, and magazines such as *Spin* plastered her picture on their covers—minus the band.

Exhausted from touring and frustrated by the attention on Stefani, the group began arguing and fighting among themselves toward the end of 1996. The situation became so stressful that No Doubt considered breaking up. They used the music video for "Don't Speak" to send a message. Stefani's energy for the song had been drawn from her breakup with Kanal, but in the video, No Doubt chose the theme of the band splitting apart. Filming the video was difficult. Stefani remembered, "We were on tour for too long and we weren't getting along. We thought the saddest thing we could do was a video about the band breaking up, 'cause we really thought we might."[17]

As it turned out, filming the video was a healthy release. It allowed the group to blow off steam and find some peace among themselves. The video depicts a sad band practice with members reminiscing about happier times. At a photo shoot for the band, the photographer takes the guys out of the shot and focuses on Stefani. She poses, but then gives sad, guilty glances at her bandmates.

No Doubt used the theme again for the video of "Excuse Me Mr." but took a humorous approach. In the scenes showing the

Tony Kanal

Tony Kanal arrived in California from England in 1981 at age eleven. His parents were from East India. He attended Anaheim High School and played saxophone in the marching band and jazz band and later took up bass. Kanal was a huge fan of Prince and attended a concert on the *Purple Rain* tour, and he was never afraid to wear purple to school.

As a high school junior, he attended a No Doubt concert and was hooked. Soon after, he tried out for the band. He had long hair and looked nothing like a ska musician, and even though he had never been in a band before, he was invited to join.

Stefani developed a crush on Kanal, and they began dating. They remained a couple for seven years. The band credits Stefani and Kanal's breakup for fueling the song "Don't Speak," which spent sixty-three weeks on *Billboard* magazine's Top 100 Airplay Chart.

Kanal remained with No Doubt until the band took a break in 2003. He has taken part in planning a reunion and a new CD for the band at an undetermined date.

entire band, Stefani, Dumont, and Kanal take turns pushing each other out of view of the camera. The scenes break away from the band and shift to Stefani being tied to railroad tracks as in an old-time movie—the rest of the band looks on but makes no moves to save her. Stefani saves herself from the oncoming train. The final scene in the video is of all four members posing together and smiling—the group's way of stating that they belonged together.

Fame, Fortune, and Fatigue

Adding to the stress in November 1996 was Stefani's health. The band had performed nearly every night for the entire year, and her voice was suffering. After shuffling a few shows, the group realized that the only option was to postpone the European tour scheduled for that month. By moving the shows to 1997, Stefani got a chance to rest her vocal cords. The band hired a voice coach to help her learn to reduce the stress caused by singing. With Stefani healthy again, they resumed touring in early 1997.

January and February kept No Doubt on the move. They played huge concerts in arenas and stadiums. The days of small, stuffy nightclubs were falling far behind them. Concerts of up to thirty thousand tickets were selling out.

The band had to take a break from the tour to attend the American Music Awards in January, where they were nominated as favorite new artist in rock/pop. A second break was needed to attend the Grammy Awards in February, where they were nominated for best new artist and best rock album. No Doubt did not win at either show, but they were excited by the nominations and the attention. In March 1997 they celebrated their tenth anniversary since their first official show at The Roxy.

Smooth Sailing

By May 1997 some of No Doubt's tougher days were behind them. The possibility of a breakup had long passed. The media were treating No Doubt like a band, not just a cute singer and some musician guys—all four of them appeared together on the cover of *Rolling Stone* magazine. *Tragic Kingdom* was selling in record

No Doubt members (left to right) Tony Kanal, Gwen Stefani, Tom Dumont, and Adrian Young celebrate their Best Group Video win at the MTV Music Awards in September 1997.

numbers; by the summer, it had sold 7 million copies. The sales of *No Doubt* had also soared; its sales numbers topped 250,000 albums. Celebrities took notice of No Doubt, and the band met George Lucas and Prince at two of its concerts.

With the arrival of autumn the band found time to wind down. In September they won the best group video award at the MTV Music Awards. They ended their lengthy tour with final stops in Europe, India, Singapore, and South America. Interscope rereleased *The Beacon Street Collection*. By winter, Stefani, Kanal, Dumont, and Young each moved into a new house in the Los Angeles area. Stefani was twenty-nine years old and moving out of her parents' house for the first time.

Tom Dumont

A member of a heavy metal band in the late 1980s, Dumont became tired of the heavy metal culture. He felt that fans were more interested in drinking, wearing tight spandex clothes, and getting crazy at concerts than they were in the music. After hearing No Doubt rehearse, he auditioned for the band and became its guitar player in 1988. Dumont's guitar playing added a kick of heavy metal to the band's ska sound.

Dumont grew up in Irvine, California, and some of his favorite bands were KISS, Judas Priest, and Iron Maiden. He spent five semesters at Orange Coast Community College studying music theory. This helped him understand how to compose music and allowed him to help the other band members learn the art of composing.

A self-proclaimed "nerd," Dumont also enjoys surfing. He handles most of the responsibility of managing the No Doubt Web site. He and his wife, Mieke, have two sons, Ace and Rio. After No Doubt took a break in 2003, Dumont played guitar with musician friends and continued working on songs for No Doubt's eventual CD.

Gwen Stefani and boyfriend Gavin Rossdale share a celebratory moment as they welcome the new millennium. Gwen was performing with No Doubt on MTV's New Year's Eve show on December 31, 1999.

The band took a break and began talking about new songs. For most of 1998 they each pursued some individual projects. Stefani sang at a benefit hosted by Don Henley and recorded a song called "You're the Boss" with Brian Setzer for his album *Dirty Boogie*. No Doubt recorded a song called "I Throw My Toys Around" for *The Rugrats Movie* soundtrack. They threw some parties and wrote new songs for their next album.

In February 1999 the group got down to business and hired Glen Ballard as their new producer. They began recording new music at two different studios in Los Angeles. As Stefani saw it, the group had three goals: "to grow as songwriters, keep it simple and clean instrumentally with no tricks, and to be spontaneous."[18] By May they had recorded seventeen songs. The new songs had a different flavor that was heavy on 1980s New Wave, with reggae, pop, and rock in the mix.

No Doubt recorded more songs over the summer and then hit the road for an eighty-city West Coast club tour at the end of September. They finished the year by performing at MTV's Times Square New Year's Eve party to say farewell to 1999.

New Millennium, New Album

More than a year in the making, No Doubt released *Return of Saturn* in January 2000. Their fame landed them on *Late Night with Conan O'Brien*, *The Tonight Show with Jay Leno*, and the cover of *Rolling Stone* magazine, and won Stefani a spot on the cover of *CosmoGirl* magazine. When asked about *Return of Saturn*, Stefani mused, "It's a selfish record in a way because the songs are largely about me—and my insecurities. I laid it all out there—and it feels good."[19]

The road for *Return of Saturn* was far smoother than the journey for *Tragic Kingdom*. No Doubt went on a month-long press tour of Europe, and Stefani was photographed for *InStyle* magazine. The rest of 2000 was like a dream. No Doubt played concerts, gave interviews, filmed videos, attended awards shows, and enjoyed the rock star life. By December *Return of Saturn* had sold more than a million copies, earning it platinum status.

No Slowing Down—Time to *Rock Steady*

Energized by the success of the previous year, No Doubt was ready to blaze ahead. In January 2001 the group began writing more songs for another album and was recording them before the month was over. Their inspiration continued into February.

In March Stefani recorded a song called "Let Me Blow Ya Mind" with rap singer Eve. In April they performed it on *Saturday Night Live* and in August at the Teen Choice Awards.

Meanwhile, No Doubt was in and out of the studio and by August settled on a name for their newest CD: *Rock Steady*. After recording more tracks in London, the group toured with the band U2 during October and November.

Rock Steady was released on December 11, 2001, and immediately landed in the Top Ten on the *Billboard* magazine album chart. On December 15 No Doubt played two of the new songs on *Saturday Night Live*. The band reveled in an amazing year jam-packed with attention, events, and terrific fun. No Doubt had hit the top of their game and hung on tightly to enjoy the ride.

Well-Deserved Success

Tragic Kingdom, *Return of Saturn*, and *Rock Steady* had launched No Doubt out of Orange County and into music history. The success of the albums and concerts practically allowed the group to write their own ticket—for their next album, next tour, or whatever the band had in mind. *Tragic Kingdom*'s sales had surpassed 10 million CDs, earning it diamond award status and locking No Doubt into the rock and roll history books.

Even as their success bubbled over, life moved on for the band members. By the beginning of 2002, Adrian Young was married and expecting his first child. Stefani had been dating Gavin Rossdale for six years. And more major news was about to break for No Doubt.

On the morning of January 1, 2002, Rossdale proposed to Stefani. She immediately said *yes*, and wedding plans got underway. With her busy schedule, she had little time to daydream about being a bride.

In February No Doubt played for Mardi Gras in New Orleans and a benefit called Concerts for Artists' Rights. Stefani then found herself with a prime seat at the 44th Annual Grammy Awards, where she presented an award—and won an award herself. Together with Eve, Stefani won best rap/song collaboration for their song "Let Me Blow Ya Mind."

Once 2002 got started, the band's success continued. No Doubt began their *Rock Steady* tour in March in Puerto Rico and then made appearances on the *Late Show with Conan O'Brien* in April and *The Tonight Show with Jay Leno* in June. In between, the band filmed the video for "Hella Good" and provided voice work for XBox and PlayStation 2 games, with Stefani serving as the voice of Malice. June came along with a chance for some fun—Stefani

Adrian Young

Drummer for No Doubt, Adrian Young grew up in Cypress, California. His early influences were Jimi Hendrix and Janis Joplin, whose records were played by his parents, as well as Deep Purple, Led Zeppelin, and The Doors. Young received his first drum kit as a Christmas gift in 1987.

Young was a huge fan of No Doubt while drumming for a group called Echostar. After playing with them for about a year, Young auditioned for No Doubt in 1989. He told the group he had been in a band for seven years, even though he had drummed with Echostar for only a year. Yet his talent impressed No Doubt, and he was invited to join.

The drummer is considered the wild man of No Doubt, and sometimes shows a hint of goth in his style, such as wearing devil horns on his head. For many years, he performed at concerts wearing only boxer shorts.

Young proposed to his girlfriend during a No Doubt concert and the couple was married in 2000. When not performing with the band, his passion is playing golf. He is married and has a son named Mason.

enjoyed a bachelorette party and bridal shower in honor of her upcoming wedding.

A few days later the band filmed a video for "Underneath It All" and then departed on a tour of Europe for a month. In August the tour took them to Honolulu, Singapore, Tokyo, and Sydney, Australia, as well as many more stops along the way. Stefani returned home only three weeks before her wedding, just in time for No Doubt to win best group video and best pop video for "Hey Baby" at the MTV Video Music Awards.

Despite the hectic schedules, Stefani had no complaints about touring. She explained:

> It's awesome. It's incredible being in a different country every day. It's my favorite thing about my success—being able to go to China, for instance, and you have this stereotype in your head of what it's going to be like, and it's not like that at all. It's this big eye-opener. You feel like the world is so big, yet so small. We're all so different, yet the same, and music is so powerful. It transcends any of that.[20]

Although she was thrilled at her opportunities for travel, Stefani was relieved to arrive in London and have a few weeks to prepare for her next big event—her upcoming wedding.

Chapter 4

The Real Life of Gwen Stefani

Gwen Stefani had experienced many thrills throughout her life—concerts, travel, award shows, adoring fans, and many other opportunities that celebrities enjoy. As much as she loved her life, her world had been all about the band ever since high school. Some exciting changes were in store for her—changes that would allow her to focus on herself and her own dreams.

A Storybook Wedding—with Pizzazz

Even with her rock star lifestyle, Stefani always considered herself very traditional about marriage, children, and family. Like many women, one of the biggest days of her life was her wedding day. On September 14, 2002, Stefani married Gavin Rossdale at St. Paul's Covent Garden Anglican Church in London. The priest who married them had been Rossdale's religious studies teacher in school. Stefani was so busy before the wedding that Rossdale handled much of the work with a wedding planner.

Stefani's wedding gown was custom designed just for her and combined a traditional white wedding gown with her own personal flair. The dress was a full-length pink and white silk gown with a flowing train designed by John Galliano. The dress had an asymmetrical neckline that was off the shoulder on one side. The back featured corset-style lacing. The most striking feature was the deep pink hemline that encircled the gown. It was created using the ombré technique—the skirting's pink color was deepest at the bottom, with the pink dye growing paler as it flowed up the skirt, until it blended perfectly with the creamy white of the upper gown.

The look was completed with a full-length sheer veil, and Stefani carried a small white orchid bouquet with ribbon streamers affixed to her grandmother's white prayer book. Stefani was hailed as a trendsetter who combined classic elegance and tradition with her own sense of style and flair.

Gavin Rossdale

Lead singer for the British grunge band Bush, Gavin Rossdale met Gwen Stefani in 1996 when No Doubt was scheduled as the opening act for Bush's concert tour. Rossdale was interested in Stefani from the moment they met, but Stefani would not date him at first. When she began to consider it, Adrian Young, Tom Dumont, and Tony Kanal forbade her from seeing Rossdale. Because he was a musician who traveled extensively with his band, Stefani's No Doubt "brothers" could not bring themselves to trust Rossdale. They changed their minds after Stefani and Rossdale's relationship began.

Rossdale married Stefani in 2002, and their son Kingston was born in 2006. Their second child, Zuma, was born in 2008.

Rossdale recorded five CDs with his band Bush and has recorded three solo albums. He filmed numerous music videos and made brief appearances in three movies, including *Zoolander*. He toured the United States and Europe over the summer of 2008.

A former tennis player, Rossdale was a schoolmate of tennis champion Roger Federer and is sometimes in attendance at Federer's tennis matches, such as the series at Wimbledon.

Gavin Rossdale and Gwen Stefani were married on September 14, 2002, at St. Paul's Covent Garden Anglican Church in London, England.

Even Stefani's arrival at the church was unique. She was driven in a beautiful blue Rolls-Royce, but was an hour late for her own ceremony.

The groom added his own personality to the ceremony. Rossdale was escorted down the aisle by his Hungarian sheepdog, Winston. The dog wore a garland of red roses for the occasion.

Following the ceremony, guests were driven on London's signature double-decker buses to a private club called Home House. About 150 guests were invited.

Two weeks later the newlyweds hosted a second wedding in Los Angeles for all of their California friends and family. Guests were instructed in the invitations to wear "romantic" clothing. Stefani again wore her pink and white gown but altered the accessories. The ceremony was a renewal of their vows and was officiated by a Catholic priest.

Stefani and Rossdale departed for a short honeymoon in Capri after the Los Angeles festivities. After their return, the couple had little time as husband and wife before Stefani was back on tour with No Doubt, including three shows with the Rolling Stones in October.

The Year to Slow Down

Already a big year, 2002 was topped off with a huge honor in November. The mayor of Anaheim, Tom Daly, presented No Doubt with the key to the city, in honor of their Anaheim roots and their tremendous success.

No Doubt had been living with jam-packed schedules since the explosive success of *Tragic Kingdom* in 1996. They had recorded two more albums, filmed several videos, and toured around the world more than once. After playing the Super Bowl in January and winning their first-ever Grammy Award for the song "Hey Baby," the group took a deep breath. They decided that a long vacation was what everyone needed most.

Stefani was looking forward to spending time with her husband. Similarly, drummer Adrian Young longed for more time with his wife and baby son. The others also felt the need for some time off, so they all agreed that they would take a break from the

Gwen Stefani laughs with host Jay Leno after an appearance with No Doubt on* The Tonight Show *in June 2002. The year 2002 was hectic for Stefani and the band.

band. None of them considered it a breakup. They all knew that the time would come when they would be ready to write, record, and go on tour again.

Stefani was ready for a break, but in her heart she had always wanted to record a solo album with styles that were different from No Doubt. She dreamed of creating music that reminded her of dance music from the 1980s. She had been writing songs for many years and felt ready to strike out in a new direction. Creative opportunities came along even before she was ready.

Next Stop: The Silver Screen

The singer's chance for a new project came along in a hurry, but it was not a new album. Stefani had been interested in acting in a movie for several years. She had tried out for a few parts, but her schedule of recording and touring with No Doubt made that process difficult.

Stefani knew that director Martin Scorsese was filming a movie called *The Aviator* with Leonardo DiCaprio, but her agent told her the film was using only big-name actors. Set in the 1930s, the movie embodied the Old Hollywood glamour that Stefani loved.

About the same time Scorsese was casting his movie, Stefani appeared on the very first cover of *Teen Vogue* magazine. The photo shoot for that magazine had been designed to match the styles of Marilyn Monroe's famous beach photos from 1949. While driving in New York City, Scorsese spotted an ad for *Teen Vogue* magazine on the side of a bus stop shelter. He asked his daughter, "Who's that girl? We should get her to try out!"[21]

When Stefani got a call to audition for the movie, she thought she might have a real shot at getting the part of actress Jean Harlow. But first, she had to audition, and that was terrifying. "My stomach was on the floor," Stefani said. "It's totally humiliating to walk in and have to try out. They know who you are, but it's a casting-call thing."[22]

Stefani was encouraged by the casting agents. They gave her suggestions for what to wear and how to perform. Soon after, she got a call to return for an audition in front of DiCaprio and Scorsese. The second audition was even more stressful, since she could hear other women trying out in the next room.

Although the part was small, consisting of only a few lines, Stefani was thrilled to get it. It gave her the chance to step into the past, directly into the shoes—and dress, hair, and makeup—of one of her biggest idols. She had wanted to act in a movie and was a huge fan of Jean Harlow, so all her dreams meshed together. She traveled to Montreal in August and Los Angeles in September 2003 for the filming.

Stefani loved the new experience, even though her scene was like something out of her own life. She said: "It was really familiar, walking down the red carpet, so it wasn't really branching out. Acting is a lot different than singing. It's not as theatrical, it's a lot more subtle, and that's a lot harder. Simpler is usually harder. So I would love to do more."[23]

The Aviator was released to theaters on December 25, 2004. It received eleven Academy Award nominations and won five Academy Awards.

Jean Harlow

Known as Hollywood's original "blond bombshell," Jean Harlow made her first movie, *Why Is a Plumber?* in 1927. She got her big break in 1930 when Howard Hughes cast her for a lead in *Hell's Angels*. She made six movies with heartthrob Clark Gable and was in high demand as a movie actress. In 1935, as her popularity grew, she changed her name to Jean Harlow, her mother's maiden name.

Harlow was born Harlean Carpenter in Kansas City, Missouri, in 1911. She married her first husband at the age of sixteen. That marriage ended in divorce, and Harlow's second husband committed suicide after being married for only two months. In 1933 she married for the third time, but that marriage lasted only eight months.

Jean Harlow made a total of thirty-six films. Some of her best-known movies are *Dinner at Eight*, *Bombshell*, and *Reckless*.

Harlow died in 1937 at the age of twenty-six. She suffered from kidney failure, which was linked to an incidence of scarlet fever during her childhood.

Jean Harlow was idolized by many women during her lifetime, and she caught the attention of young Gwen Stefani. Along with Marilyn Monroe, Stefani had a fascination for Harlow. Playing Jean Harlow in the 2004 film *The Aviator* was a dream come true for Stefani.

Gwen Stefani had a small role playing Jean Harlow in the movie* The Aviator. *The star of the film was Leonardo DiCaprio, shown here with Stefani attending the Los Angeles premier in December 2004.

The Launch of L.A.M.B. Clothing

Whether Stefani was onstage, appearing in a movie or video, or just going shopping, fashion was important to her. Experimenting with clothes was as natural for Stefani as breathing. After years of designing clothes for the stage and music videos, as well as her personal wardrobe, her stylist prompted an idea. Stefani explains:

> My stylist, Andrea Lieberman, and I were making so many outfits, we decided, Why don't we do a clothing line together? It's every girl's dream. We were going to do something really small and just sell our stuff at a few boutiques, and then I met this guy who said he wanted to do a clothing line with me and pay for everything. The best part was he said I could do whatever I wanted creatively. I was like, *Are you kidding? Okay*.[24]

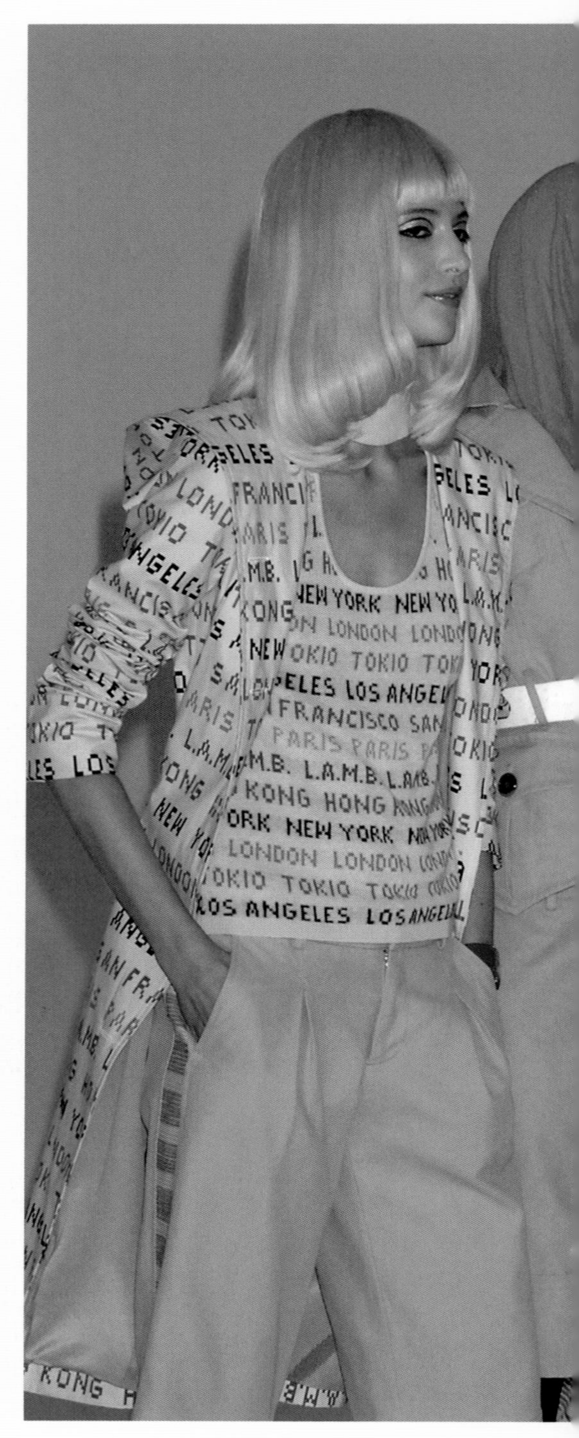

Gwen Stefani (dressed in black) poses with models during Stefani's L.A.M.B. Spring 2007 Collection show in September 2006. An assortment of Stefani's favorite styles were part of the L.A.M.B. collection.

In September 2003, about the same time she was filming *The Aviator*, that fashion dream came true. Stefani launched a line of handbags and accessories under her new fashion label called L.A.M.B. It stood for Love. Angel. Music. Baby. and would become a phrase that Stefani would use repeatedly. The bags were mostly black, with handles that resembled guitar straps. The bags were an instant hit and sold quickly.

In the spring of 2004, L.A.M.B released its first clothing line. Stefani described the clothes: "It's basically the clothes I wear. I want it to be my style, so I can wear them. I don't know what it will evolve into. . . . I'm still learning. It's just another creative thing for me to do, and it's exciting."[25]

The L.A.M.B collection began as an assortment of Stefani's favorite styles going back about ten years. It included T-shirts, destroy-washed jeans, and a halter dress reminiscent of a dress worn by Marilyn Monroe. The clothes caught the attention of celebrities such as Hilary Duff, Sandra Bullock, and Carmen Electra. Within a few years, the collection expanded to include CD and iPod cases, tote bags, wallets, and shoes. Some items were adorned with Stefani's lyrics.

The goal of the company was to produce clothes for teens and young women with a classic yet updated feel. For her spring collection in 2008, many of the shapes were form fitting and evoked the mood of the 1950s, 1960s, and 1970s. The palette was predominantly black, white, and gray, but with patterns, splashes of color, and designs to make them modern and trendy.

"The simple reason that I started L.A.M.B.," Stefani revealed, "was to have something really creative in my life other than music. 'Cause I don't know what's going to happen. I want to be prepared [in case my music career ends]. I'm very passionate and I never get tired, but I never thought I was going to get this deep. I pinch myself every day."[26]

Stefani credited her mother for supporting her fashion endeavors ever since she was young. She said she considered the clothing line "a connection to my mom because we always sewed together."[27] When Stefani told her mother that she was going to appear in *Vogue* magazine with her clothing line, her mother cried with excitement.

A Compact Disc of Her Own

In between filming *The Aviator* and launching L.A.M.B. clothing, Stefani talked about new music with Tony Kanal. They thought that a new CD with the sound of 1980s dance music would be fast and easy to put together. They tossed around ideas and styles that included Prince, the Time, Madonna, and Club Nouveau. As ideas kept coming, though, the project became larger and more difficult than they ever expected.

Being married presented a new challenge as well. Stefani told *Cosmopolitan*: "It's been hard to focus. Coming off the tour and having my first year of being married. I'm kind of lazy. I like to lie around with my husband and watch TV and stuff like that. It takes a lot of selfish time to make music."[28] For the first time Stefani was torn between working on her CD and spending time with her new husband.

Stefani was also alone with her music—something she had never done before. In the past she had the band members of No Doubt to support her and write songs with her. As a team they all contributed to the band's music and produced impressive results. Working without her team was harder than she expected.

Jimmy Iovine, who produced No Doubt's albums for Interscope Records, encouraged Stefani to attempt the solo album. He paired her with Linda Perry, a singer, songwriter, and producer. Perry had worked with Christina Aguilera, Pink, Alicia Keys, and many other artists. Iovine had confidence in Stefani. He recalls, "She was nervous about it. It was her first time doing something without her band, and it was a big step. I said, 'Let's just experiment and see what happens.'"[29]

Trying to be creative on her own made Stefani feel vulnerable. "It was very threatening to let these people into my world," she says. "Because that's what I define myself as—a songwriter. The hardest part was letting someone even suggest an idea and then my ego being able to take it if it was good."[30]

On their first day of working together, Stefani and Perry wrote an entire song called "Fine by You." Stefani went home at the end of the day feeling proud and happy at their accomplishment. The next morning, Stefani discovered that Perry had been up all night and had written a song called "What You Waiting For?" Perry had seen Stefani's talent and could not understand why she was holding back. The song was Perry's way of nudging Stefani to jump into songwriting and let her creativity run free.

Breaking New Ground

Stefani felt pangs of jealousy at Perry's ability to write music. That jealousy motivated Stefani and pushed her to write more and try harder. "It was like a dare, and I don't even remember writing the words," she said. "I just barfed them out."[31]

As Stefani became more comfortable with the album, she allowed her creativity to pour forth. She became determined to dedicate a song to the Japanese Harajuku girls, whom she had seen during her trip to Tokyo with No Doubt in 1996. She explained: "Everyone had this crazy personal style. All these different things like gothic Lolitas and girls with blond hair and dark tans and high heels, like they were from Hollywood."[32]

Love. Angel. Music. Baby.

By working with Linda Perry, Tony Kanal, and more than a dozen others, the songs for Stefani's album were eventually finished. The CD was titled *Love. Angel. Music. Baby.* The initials spelled the word *L.A.M.B.* and mirrored the name of her clothing line, and the phrase was actually a secret reference to her dog Marilyn.

The CD was released in November 2004. Music critics gave tough reviews, finding the lyrics to be too simplistic. They felt the album did not have a cohesive theme to hold it together, and the songs were too much of a hodgepodge of different musical styles. Because Stefani collaborated with more than a dozen different people in writing the songs, the critics felt the true Gwen Stefani was lost in the jumble. The critics admitted, though, that the album was enjoyable to listen and dance to and contained a fun mix of tunes.

In her own way Stefani agreed with the critics. She told *Blender* magazine, "Everyone keeps calling it a solo record and I keep calling it a dance record. 'Cause if I was doing a solo record, that would be like, finally, *me* . . . finally this is the real Gwen Stefani. It's not that.

Gwen Stefani celebrates the release of her solo album Love. Angel. Music. Baby. *in November 2004. Although Stefani partially agreed with the critics who gave the album tough reviews, the CD became a huge hit.*

This album is actually *less* of me than I've ever been before."[33]

Fans had different opinions from the critics. The CD was a hit, and it reached gold and platinum status in less than a month. After six months *Love. Angel. Music. Baby.* reached multiplatinum, and within days of its first anniversary, the album had sold 3 million copies, certifying it as triple multiplatinum.

The most popular song on the album was "Hollaback Girl," a high school–themed tune with a driving dance beat. As a single, it also reached gold and platinum status. The songs "Rich Girl" and "What You Waiting For?" followed closely behind. Both became gold certified for Stefani.

The singer's reaction to the success of the album was repeated over and over throughout her career: surprise. Just as she had experienced with No Doubt, she was amazed that her album was something so many people wanted to buy. When she went on tour to promote the CD, she was amazed again that her concerts sold out and that so many fans lined up to hear her music.

Stefani's Own Harajuku Girls

As she was writing the song "Harajuku Girls," Stefani got the idea to create actual Harajuku Girls to help promote the album. She hired four dancers to perform onstage with her and also to appear along with her during interviews and promotions. The job of the dancers was to look

Gwen Stefani included her own Harajuku Girls in her 2005 tour. She first became aware of their style when No Doubt visited Tokyo in 1996.

cute and wear the trendiest Japanese Harajuku fashions. Pictures of the dancers are sprinkled throughout the artwork in the liner notes of the CD.

Stefani described the Harajuku Girls as a figment of her imagination brought to life. She considered the girls to be culturally positive and an art project—something fun to add to her music. Stefani named the four Harajuku Girls Love, Angel, Music, and Baby.

The Harajuku Girls sparked unexpected controversy. Comedian Margaret Cho, a Korean American, and Jonathan Ross, a British TV host, made jokes about the Harajuku Girls. They suggested that Stefani was promoting a negative stereotype of Japanese women. Cho later apologized for her remarks, admitting that she had not bothered to understand why Stefani had added the Harajuku Girls to her performances.

Stefani was surprised by the racist reactions she received but refused to give up the Harajuku Girls. She had always considered them to be an element of fun—just another way to add different styles to her concerts and videos. Her determination was another example of her ability to resist pressure and stay true to herself.

The Highs and Lows of Fame

Despite her fame and success, Stefani still felt like an ordinary girl from Orange County. Yet she truly appreciated the good fortune in her life. She says, "I'm lucky not to have a real job, to be able to express myself, be creative, and be relevant. I don't know what I will be doing in ten years."[34]

Stefani had come a long way and had learned many things about music, recording, and touring. Yet every once in a while, a hard lesson still came along. Stefani was blindsided by reporters from *Spin* and *Face* magazines when they asked whether she had lost her virginity to Tony Kanal. Stefani, with her Catholic background, was horrified that they would ask such a question. She replied:

> I would never tell you that! Are you crazy? I would never tell anyone that. I have pretty strong feelings about that. If any girls were to ask me what my advice would be, completely wait as long as possible, wait till you're married. I

> think it's really a sacred thing. It's different when you get older and have a boyfriend. . . . It's such a blessing that God gave us—we should be able to respect it. I'm not going to talk about that stuff any more.[35]

The situation made Stefani wish that reporters would stick with topics like her music and her fashion.

Another Fashion Venture—Harajuku Lovers

Stefani's L.A.M.B. clothing line had exploded on the fashion scene. It was enjoying huge popularity and sales beyond anyone's expectations. As a result, Stefani saw another opportunity to share

Harajuku Girls

While on tour in Japan with No Doubt in 1996, Stefani fell in love with the mix-and-match fashion of the young women in Japan, and she discovered the style known as Harajuku. The style was named for the Harajuku district of Tokyo. Girls in that area developed a unique style that blended school uniforms, ruffled miniskirts, short petticoats or crinolines, bright colors, and artistic makeup and hairstyles. The style is also sometimes called "gothic Lolita," because it incorporates little-girl clothes with spiky hair, punk shoes, leather dog collars, and other elements of the goth look.

Stefani never forgot the look of Harajuku and began weaving elements of the style into her wardrobe. Even years later, when writing songs for her first CD, she liked it so much that she wrote a song called "Harajuku Girls." She also hired four young women to wear the style and serve as dancers in her videos and on her tours. One of their appearances was in the "Wind It Up" video, in which they appeared as the von Trapp family children.

her passions with the rest of the world. She launched a line of accessories in 2005 called Harajuku Lovers with the purpose of making new items available to fans of the style. With the Japanese styles not readily available in the United States, the new line provided a source for the hard-to-find look.

The new items quickly gained popularity and featured watches, backpacks, tote bags, T-shirts, tank tops, shorts, and sweat pants for women and girls. The designs included bright colors and pastels; cartoon characters; and bold, whimsical patterns. Stefani established a new Web site for the Harajuku Lovers line in order for fans to have access to the merchandise from anywhere in the world.

Chapter 5

The Sound of Gwen Stefani's Music

Stefani had enjoyed huge successes for several years, but she was in for another happy surprise during the first week of October 2005. That week she learned that she had made music history. The song "Hollaback Girl" became the first downloaded song ever to sell 1 million downloads. Shortly thereafter, the song also crossed the 1 million mark in mobile telephone downloads. Stefani was humbled by the milestone. She said: "It's always an honor to be recognized for your music, and this is really the coolest. It's exciting to see people embrace the song and really make it part of their lives. Whether it's CDs, computers, or cell phones . . . it really is bananas."[36]

Days after the news of her record-breaking downloads, Stefani began her concert tour in Phoenix, Arizona. Over the next twenty-six days, she performed in nineteen cities from coast to coast. The event was known as the *Harajuku Lovers* tour, taking its identity from Stefani's dancers. The band Black Eyed Peas traveled with her as the opening act of the concerts. Another ten concerts in nine cities followed, featuring M.I.A. as the opening band.

In December 2005 Stefani's tour visited an additional twelve cities throughout the United States and Canada. Artist Ciara joined the tour as the opening act.

A New Member of the Family

Concert tours are known to be strenuous and exhausting, but Stefani was faced with a special challenge. Shortly before beginning

Gwen Stefani's baby boy, Kingston James McGregor Rossdale, was born in Los Angeles on May 26, 2006.

her 2005 tour, she learned that she was pregnant. Stefani was thrilled, but the demands of being pregnant while on tour almost got the best of her. She explains:

> I'd be crying before I was going on. I couldn't breathe, because when you're pregnant, you get short of breath. So I'm trying to breathe with the corset and the high heels and the nine costume changes. I was in pain. I had really bad stomach aches. What saved me was God put these young girls in the front row. You could tell it was their first concert and they were looking at me as if I was Cinderella. They just thought I was great.[37]

Stefani was glad to see the tour end and get some much-needed rest. The following spring, on May 26, 2006, her son was born in Los Angeles, weighing 7.5 pounds (3.4kg). Stefani and her husband named him Kingston James McGregor Rossdale. Over the next several months, the proud parents spent as much time with their son as they could. Baby Kingston learned to travel at a very young age.

Stefani had known that she wanted to be a mom ever since she was a little girl. Before the band came along, she used to fantasize about getting married and having children. With Kingston's arrival, motherhood felt completely normal and natural. Observers noted that Stefani handled a diaper bag and stroller as easily as a microphone.

The Sweet Escape

Even Kingston's arrival did not stop Stefani from getting back to work. She had started writing songs for another CD the previous fall, before the *Harajuku Lovers* tour began. Stefani explains:

> In September 2005, [record producer] Pharrell Williams called me and said, "Come down to Miami and make some records." I was not really pursuing making a record, but how do you turn him down? In ten days, we came up with "Breakin' Up," "Orange County Girl," and "Wind It Up." Then after [the *Harajuku Girls* tour], I went in with Tony,

> and we got "Don't Get It Twisted" and "4 in the Morning" going. So at that point, I realized I could get a record out by Christmas, but then I found out I was going to have Kingston. After Kingston, I went back into the studio again. "Early Winter" I did with Tim [Rice-Oxley], and I also went in with Akon and Sean Garrett.[38]

For her CD in progress, Stefani also rescued two songs that never made it onto *Love. Angel. Music. Baby.* She remembered: "They were burning up my iTunes, so I thought, 'Are these really just going to sit on my computer?' 'Wonderful Life' I wrote for a friend who passed away, and it didn't really fit on the first record. 'U Started It' was a song I wrote the day before I wrote 'Hollaback Girl,' so I didn't put that one on either, even though it broke my heart."[39]

Her second CD, titled *The Sweet Escape*, arrived in stores on December 5, 2006. The night before its release, Stefani appeared on the 2006 Billboard Music Awards and performed the song "Wind It Up."

"Wind It Up" caused a huge buzz among fans and critics. The song borrowed music and lyrics from a tune called "The Lonely Goatherd" from *The Sound of Music*. Stefani even yodeled a few lines, as was done in the movie. Stefani's dancers onstage and in the video appeared in costumes that mimicked the children's play clothes from the movie. The fabric for those costumes featured a geometric "GS" pattern (Stefani's initials) that imitated the cream and olive green drapery fabric that was used to make the outfits in the movie.

Reviews of *The Sweet Escape* were mixed. Some critics hated the yodeling and found many of the songs to be uninteresting. Others loved certain sounds or styles. Many critics disagreed as to which were the best songs on the album.

Nonetheless, Stefani was pleased with the CD and made no apologies for its unusual elements. She said: "It's definitely left of center. Yodeling is not very fashionable. I agree that you take a bite [of 'Wind It Up'] and it's like, 'What? This tastes weird.' But after a few bites, you're addicted. I understand [the mixed reactions]. I picked it on purpose. That's why it's called *The Sweet Escape*—it is supposed to be fun, easy-to-go-down music."[40] Stefani's fans embraced her album, eager once again to find out what she had dished up, and the CD sold well. Her next new venture would also turn out to be an instant hit.

Never Too Old for Dolls

Having been compared to a Barbie doll at least once, the idea of turning Stefani into a line of fashion dolls probably came naturally. In December 2006 Stefani worked with Huckleberry Toys to release a series of eight dolls resembling herself and her Harajuku Girl dancers. The 10-inch (25cm) dolls resembled fashion dolls, and their costumes were replicated from her *Harajuku Lovers* tour. Stefani explained on her Web site: "I thought the dolls would be a good opportunity to capture some of the key looks from the album and the tour. The Harajuku Girls and I wore such wicked costumes we had to share them with the world again."[41]

The dolls retailed for about twenty-five dollars each and included Cool Gwen in a glamorous gown, Tick Tock Gwen sporting an Alice in Wonderland dress, Bananas Gwen wearing a marching band uniform, and Hollaback Gwen in Stefani's signature baggy pants and white tank top. Her Harajuku Girls were transformed into dolls as well: Love, Angel, Music, and Baby were created wearing typical Harajuku outfits such as miniskirts with petticoats.

A second series of dolls was launched in conjunction with *The Sweet Escape* tour. The set contained five dolls: Harajuku Gwen wearing a dance outfit from the video for "Wind It Up"; Orange County Girl Gwen in black pants and a black-and-white striped top; Wind It Up Gwen wearing a drapery-fabric mini trench coat; Wonderful Life Gwen sporting a plaid miniskirt and vest; and Yummy Gwen in a black sweater and animal-print shorts. The dolls quickly became scarce and sold out in stores but remained available through online sources such as Amazon.com.

The final Gwen Stefani doll was produced as a limited edition collectible for the San Diego ComicCon in 2007. The doll was dressed in a black blouse and pants and featured an additional black-and-white dress. The dolls sold out at the convention and quickly became a high-priced collectible. They left fans wanting more, yet Stefani did not release information about any more upcoming dolls.

On the Road with Kingston

In April 2007 Stefani kicked off *The Sweet Escape* tour in Las Vegas, visiting more than eighty cities in about six months. The tour wrapped around the world, with Stefani performing in Canada, Mexico, Puerto Rico, Colombia, New Zealand, Australia, Japan, China, Thailand, and many countries in Europe. Artists Akon and Lady Sovereign traveled along on the tour as guest performers.

Kingston, his crib, and his stuffed animals toured along with Stefani. Having him along made the tour more fun for her. He celebrated his first birthday in New York with his parents and grandparents while the tour was in full swing, and he was at the age when he was beginning to sing a little. "He's just getting into music," his mother said at the time. "He does the whole head-bouncing thing."[42]

The tour was made possible for Kingston with the aid of the family's nanny and frequent visits from Stefani's husband, Gavin Rossdale. With his own obligations to his band, Rossdale joined Stefani and Kingston on tour anytime he could break away.

Two months into her tour, Stefani received exciting news: *The Sweet Escape* had sold enough copies to qualify for gold and platinum awards. Stefani and her son traveled for five more months, with Rossdale joining them as schedules permitted. The family returned home to Los Angeles in November 2007.

A Scent of Her Own

In October 2007 Stefani achieved another milestone in her fashion-driven life. Her signature fragrance, called simply L, was released to stores. Packaged in shiny gold boxes, the bottles featured an iridescent rainbow flowing from red to orange to yellow to green. The fragrance itself was a blend of rose, sweet pea, lily of the valley, fresh pear, orange blossom, and musk.

"I just wanted something timeless. It just felt really right . . . it felt really *me*,"[43] Stefani said. Her goal was to create a scent that

Stefani's son Kingston traveled with her on **The Sweet Escape** *tour.*

Gold and Platinum Records

The Recording Industry Association of America (RIAA) is an organization that represents U.S. artists and record companies. In 1958 it set the standard for the gold award, which was designed as a tool to measure the sales and success of a record. A gold award was presented after an album sold more than five hundred thousand copies. In 1976 the platinum award was instituted to recognize sales of 1 million copies. As the recording industry grew after the introduction of CDs, the multiplatinum award was established in 1984 to reward sales of 2 million or more copies.

In 1999 the RIAA again expanded its criteria to recognize sales of 10 million or more albums. Known as the diamond award, approximately 103 albums have been granted this recognition. No Doubt's *Tragic Kingdom* album achieved diamond award status in 1999, less than four years after its release.

reminded her of her mother's garden, and Stefani noted that it was one of the most fun things she had ever done.

If I Were a Rich Girl— I Would Give Some Away

Like many celebrities, Stefani has looked for ways to help others with her earnings from CDs and concerts. She has been a supporter of 21st Century Leaders, Children's Hospital of Orange County, EB Medical Research Foundation, Orangewood Children's Foundation, Save the Children, UNICEF, and Whatever It Takes.

In 2007, while on *The Sweet Escape* tour, she considered canceling her show in San Diego. At that time, wildfires were consuming thousands of acres of California and had destroyed around two thousand homes. Stefani felt that canceling the concert would show respect for the many people whose lives were turned upside down by the fires. Instead, she performed as scheduled and donated the proceeds, approximately $160,000, to help victims of the fires. In December 2007 she established the Gwen Stefani After-the-Fires Scholarship for students who lost their homes or sources of income due to fire.

Stefani discovered that works for charity could be fun as well as artistic. In 2008 she became one of dozens of celebrities to contribute a design for a plate and mug sold by the nonprofit group Whatever It Takes. Stefani's design was produced on a limited number of plates and mugs and sold by the organization. The

Gwen Stefani and her No Doubt bandmates performed at the Music for Relief tsunami benefit concert in February 2005. Stefani supports numerous charities and appears at many benefits and charity balls.

proceeds from sales were contributed to the charity 21st Century Leaders.

Stefani also held two charity auctions on eBay, one in 2007 and another in 2008. Many items from her tours, including sets and costumes, plus some of her red-carpet gowns, were offered for auction. The proceeds were donated to Children's Hospital of Orange County and Orangewood Children's Foundation.

The singer has attended numerous benefits and charity balls and has performed at a number of such events. In 2005 No Doubt played at a concert to raise money for victims of the tsunami in South Asia. In 2007 she sang for *American Idol* fans on *Idol Gives Back*, which raised $75 million for humanitarian causes in the United States and Africa.

A New Addition

Even though Stefani was taking some time off in 2007, her life would not lie idle for very long. In January 2008 she announced that she was again expecting a baby. She continued to make public appearances but stayed away from touring. Being pregnant on her first solo tour had been so difficult that she vowed never to do it again.

Stefani and Rossdale's second son was born on August 21, 2008, in Los Angeles. The baby weighed 8 pounds, 5 ounces (3.77kg) and was named Zuma Nesta Rock Rossdale. Various media sources speculated about his unusual name, but Stefani gave no official explanation for the choice. The media also began speculating about when Stefani might be ready to rejoin No Doubt for a CD or concert tour.

No Doubt Reunion

No Doubt never announced a breakup or the end of the band. When they took a vacation, they intended to get back to recording and touring someday. In 2007 and 2008 Dumont, Kanal, and Young again began writing songs for a potential CD. Late in 2007 the group began spending a little time in a recording studio to work on new material.

Gavin Rossdale, Gwen Stefani, and their young son Kingston stroll in Los Angeles. Stefani and her husband welcomed another son, Zuma Nesta Rock Rossdale, on August 21, 2008.

Gwen Stefani's fashion signature for years has been bright blond hair and bright red lipstick.

After learning of Stefani's pregnancy, the band decided to move slowly. Recording was postponed to take place after the arrival of her baby. A release date and title were not announced for the CD, but the band was looking forward to reuniting as a group. In the No Doubt Web site journals, Adrian Young wrote a blog about the band joining Stefani's concert encores in California in June 2007. He wrote that the band had a blast and the fans went crazy. For No Doubt, the question of reuniting was never a matter of *if*, but a matter of *when*.

What Could Be Missing?

With all of her success, it is difficult to imagine that Stefani might see anything missing in her life. Yet one thing in particular has eluded her.

Stefani says: "I would love to learn to play something so I don't have to rely on someone to collaborate with. I've written songs on guitar, but I don't play guitar good enough to be free. If I could play every chord? I could write a million songs if I had that."[44]

Stefani's Fashion-Forward Philosophy

Marching bands, dancing Harajuku Girls, and yodeling have given Stefani a place for herself as a trendsetter and a unique presence in the music world. But her flair and style have not been confined to CD covers or music videos, or even to her clothing lines. Stefani's fashion choices have been watched closely and imitated by magazines, style experts, and fans.

For more than ten years, Stefani's signature look centered on her platinum blond hair and the bright red lipstick she wears anytime she is out in public. She first wanted to go blond when she was a teenager. She said, "I'd always wanted to go blond at school, but I never had the money, because you have to keep getting it done."[45] In recent years she considered changing her hair to brown, but decided that she loved her blond hair and planned to keep it that way for as long as it works for her look. As for her makeup,

Stefani makes sure she looks good any time she leaves the house. "There's always paparazzi outside my house," she explains. "If you had paparazzi outside your house, you'd make sure you looked good, too."[46]

A Best-Dressed Regular

Stefani's attention to style has repeatedly earned her the respect of the fashion community. Whereas some celebrities have been criticized for being sloppy, having no sense of style, or suffering from "wardrobe malfunctions," Stefani has been recognized many times as a fashion leader. She has been named to the best-dressed lists of *People*, *Vanity Fair*, *Harpers & Queen*, *UK Glamour*, and others. Those magazines have recognized her as someone worth watching and have described her as original, innovative, creative, and elegant.

Fans and critics alike can see that Stefani's looks are always polished and put together. Even while watching a tennis match in the hot sun at Wimbledon in 2008, Stefani, who was eight months pregnant, looked like a rock star in a long red, black, and white dress and black leather jacket.

A Real-Life Moment

A life like Gwen Stefani's might seem picture perfect, but even rock stars have messy moments. The No Doubt Web site relates one of Stefani's most unglamorous encounters. During a recording session, her fourteen-year-old dog, Maggen, pooped on the floor of the studio. Stefani cleaned it up with paper towels and took the mess outside to the trash bins. Not paying attention to doors and gates, she locked herself into the trash enclosure. With everyone else inside a soundproof studio, Stefani was trapped on top of smelly garbage cans. The evening was a giant leap from the more familiar scenes of Stefani onstage or on the red carpet at award shows.

Stefani has consistently been recognized as a fashion leader. While eight months pregnant and under the hot sun, she was a fashion-conscious spectator at the 2008 Wimbledon Tennis Championships in England.

Although she makes it look easy, Stefani has readily admitted that looking good takes a lot of work. She has a stylist, makeup artist, hair stylist, and personal trainer. Keeping her figure requires constant attention. "I have to work out really, really hard to be as hot as I am. It's difficult for me," she admits. "I think I went on my first diet in sixth grade. It's in my genes to be a little bigger and I don't like that, admittedly. I want girls to know that I work at it—it's not easy, and it doesn't come naturally, unfortunately."[47]

She also admits that she is far from perfect when it comes to healthy eating: "Whenever I go on a diet and get myself incredibly healthy and hot looking, I start to go, 'Oh, I look cute, let's have some pizza.' And then the whole cycle begins again."[48]

Having Fun with Fame

Some celebrities seem to lose their sense of humor after becoming rich or famous. Others seem to forget what life was like before their success. Stefani somehow remains grounded—a real person amidst the plastic and empty-headed figures sometimes found in Hollywood. For Stefani, a fancy house, expensive car, or incredible wardrobe are not the first things she appreciates. She says: "I always thought that I was going to be this perfect wife and mom. I fantasized about it for so long, and I'm not very good at

Gwen Stefani performs "Wind It Up" at the 2006 American Music Awards. Her love for the movie The Sound of Music *figures into the song: Yodeling and dancers dressed as the von Trapp children are featured.*

cleaning up and doing the homemaker thing. The one thing that makes me feel super lucky about my financial success is that I have a housekeeper. And if that ever got taken away, I would be really, really, really bummed."[49]

Stefani's sense of fun shines through in a tale she related to *Cosmopolitan*: "I was driving down Hollywood Boulevard one day and I saw this guy wearing an old No Doubt shirt, so I knew he was a die-hard fan. I rolled down the window, and I yelled to him, 'Hey, cool shirt.' He was probably nineteen. The guy seriously nearly fell over. He totally tripped. It was so cute."[50]

How Do You Solve a Problem Like—Gwen?

In the movie *The Sound of Music*, the nuns sang a lighthearted song about Maria, the young nun they all loved but who was not very good at being a nun. The song described her energy, her spirit, and her sweetness, and the sentiment could certainly be applied to Gwen Stefani. She stated on many occasions that she found parallels between herself and Maria.

On the opposite end of the music spectrum is an equally appropriate song to describe Stefani's personality. The lyrics from the song "Baggy Trousers" by the band Madness, the very song that hooked her on ska music, also describe Stefani's attitudes throughout her life. Stefani managed to follow her heart, even though it meant going against current trends, and to turn her life in the direction she wanted it to go.

Stefani may seem to have landed in a perfect life, but none of it fell into her lap. She worked hard with No Doubt and struggled though many rough times. Beneath all the glitz and glamour is an energetic, tough-spirited wife, mom, and rock star who is really an Orange County girl at heart.

Introduction: Never Any Doubt

1. Quoted in No Doubt, "Timeline." www.nodoubt.com/band.

Chapter 1: Orange County Girl

2. Quoted in *People*, "Gwen Stefani: Five Fun Facts." www.people.com/people/gwen_stefani.
3. Quoted in Jonathan Cohen, "The Sound of Gwen," *Billboard*, December 16, 2006.
4. Quoted in Clark Collis, "The Good Girl," *Entertainment Weekly*, December 1, 2006.

Chapter 2: Not Just Luck

5. Quoted in Amy Blankstein, *Omnibus Press Presents the Story of Gwen Stefani*. London: Omnibus, 2005, p. 20.
6. Quoted in Blankstein, *Omnibus Press Presents the Story of Gwen Stefani*, p. 21.
7. Quoted in Wendy Hermanson, "Just a Girl . . . Anaheim's No Doubt Sets the 'Rock Feminist' Label on Its Head," *BAM*, November 17, 1995. http://nodoubt1986.blogspot.com/1995/11/just-girl-anaheims-no-doubt-sets-rock.html.
8. Quoted in Hermanson, "Just a Girl . . . Anaheim's No Doubt Sets the 'Rock Feminist' Label on Its Head."
9. Quoted in Blankstein, *Omnibus Press Presents the Story of Gwen Stefani*, p. 27.
10. Quoted in No Doubt, "Timeline."
11. Quoted in Blankstein, *Omnibus Press Presents the Story of Gwen Stefani*, p. 31.
12. Quoted in *Cosmopolitan*, "It's Good to Be Gwen Stefani." www.cosmopolitan.com/celebrities/exclusive/gwen-stefani-04?click=main_sr.

Chapter 3: A New Spark for No Doubt

13. Quoted in Blankstein, *Omnibus Press Presents the Story of Gwen Stefani*, p. 33.
14. Quoted in Blankstein, *Omnibus Press Presents the Story of Gwen Stefani*, p. 33.
15. Quoted in Blankstein, *Omnibus Press Presents the Story of Gwen Stefani*, p. 34.
16. Quoted in Blankstein, *Omnibus Press Presents the Story of Gwen Stefani*, p. 40.
17. Quoted in Blankstein, *Omnibus Press Presents the Story of Gwen Stefani*, p. 42.
18. Quoted in No Doubt, "Timeline."
19. Quoted on No Doubt, "Timeline."
20. Quoted in Emma Sloley, "The Reign of Cool," *Flare*, April 2008.

Chapter 4: The Real Life of Gwen Stefani

21. Quoted in Jennifer Vineyard, "Gwen Stefani Says Acting Is a Lot Harder than Singing," MTV.com, December 2, 2004. www.mtv.com/movies/news/articles/1494427/20041202/story.jhtml.
22. Quoted in Vineyard, "Gwen Stefani Says Acting Is a Lot Harder than Singing."
23. Quoted in Vineyard, "Gwen Stefani Says Acting Is a Lot Harder than Singing."
24. Quoted in *Cosmopolitan*, "It's Good to Be Gwen Stefani."
25. Quoted in Blankstein, *Omnibus Press Presents the Story of Gwen Stefani*, p. 87.
26. Quoted in Sloley, "The Reign of Cool."
27. Quoted in Sloley, "The Reign of Cool."
28. Quoted in *Cosmopolitan*, "It's Good to Be Gwen Stefani."
29. Quoted in Jenny Eliscu, "I'll Cry Just Talking About It," Guardian.co.uk. http://arts.guardian.co.uk/print/0,,5113840 110428,00.html.

30. Quoted in Eliscu, "I'll Cry Just Talking About It."
31. Quoted in Eliscu, "I'll Cry Just Talking About It."
32. Quoted in Eliscu, "I'll Cry Just Talking About It."
33. Quoted in Ariel Levy, "The Coronation of Gwen Stefani," *Blender*, December 2004. www.blender.com/guide/articles.aspx?id=1329.
34. Quoted in Eliscu, "I'll Cry Just Talking About It."
35. Quoted in Blankstein, *Omnibus Press Presents the Story of Gwen Stefani*, p. 43.

Chapter 5: The Sound of Gwen Stefani's Music

36. Quoted in Universal Music Group, "The Future of Music Achieves Major Landmark as Gwen Stefani Makes Digital History with One Millionth Commercial Download of 'Hollaback Girl.'" http://new.umusic.com/News.aspx?NewsId=327.
37. Quoted in Clark Collis, "The Good Girl," *Entertainment Weekly*, December 1, 2006.
38. Quoted in Jonathan Cohen, "The Sound of Gwen," *Billboard*, December 16, 2006.
39. Quoted in Cohen, "The Sound of Gwen."
40. Quoted in Cohen, "The Sound of Gwen."
41. Quoted in Gwen Stefani Official Web site. www.gwenstefani.com/news/?nid=6630.
42. Quoted in Stephen M. Silverman, "Gwen Stefani Can't Wait to Get Pregnant Again," *People*. August 16, 2007. www.people.com/people/article/ 0,,20051883,00.html.
43. Quoted in L.A.M.B. Fragrance by Gwen Stefani (Gallery; Behind the Scenes). www.lambfragrance.com.
44. Quoted in Eliscu, "I'll Cry Just Talking About It."
45. Quoted in Alix Sharkey, "My Fair Lady," *Harper's Bazaar*, May 2007.
46. Quoted in Sharkey, "My Fair Lady."
47. Quoted in *Cosmopolitan*, "It's Good to Be Gwen Stefani."

48. Quoted in *Cosmopolitan*, “It’s Good to Be Gwen Stefani.”
49. Quoted in *Cosmopolitan*, “It’s Good to Be Gwen Stefani.”
50. Quoted in *Cosmopolitan*, “It’s Good to Be Gwen Stefani.”

Important Dates

1969

Gwen Stefani is born in Fullerton, California, on October 3.

1986

Eric Stefani and John Spence assemble a band and name it No Doubt; they play their first party on New Year's Eve.

1987

Stefani graduates from Loara High School and enrolls at California State Fullerton; in March No Doubt plays its most important gig to date at The Roxy on the Sunset Strip; John Spence commits suicide in an Anaheim park on December 21.

1992

No Doubt releases its first album, titled *No Doubt*; it sells thirty thousand copies, a disappointment for the record company.

1995

In March No Doubt releases its second album, *The Beacon Street Collection*; on October 6 No Doubt releases its third album, *Tragic Kingdom*; Stefani meets Gavin Rossdale, lead singer of Bush, while touring with No Doubt; shortly thereafter, they begin dating.

1996

Tragic Kingdom achieves gold award status on June 26 by selling five hundred thousand copies; Stefani visits Tokyo with No Doubt and discovers the Harajuku shopping district for the first time; she falls in love with the styles of the district and maintains her interest for many years to come; on August 21 *Tragic Kingdom* receives platinum and multiplatinum award status.

1999

No Doubt's *Tragic Kingdom* album is recognized on February 5 with diamond award status after selling 10 million copies.

2000

No Doubt issues its fourth album, *Return of Saturn*; the album achieves platinum award status on May 31.

2001

No Doubt releases its fifth album, *Rock Steady*.

2002

Stefani marries Gavin Rossdale on September 14; on October 11 *Rock Steady* achieves multiplatinum award status.

2003

No Doubt is exhausted, and the band agrees to take a break.

2004

In the spring Stefani launches her new clothing label, L.A.M.B.; Stefani's first solo CD, *Love. Angel. Music. Baby.*, is released on November 23; Stefani appears as Jean Harlow in the Martin Scorsese film *The Aviator*.

2005

"Hollaback Girl" becomes the first downloaded song ever to sell 1 million downloads; Stefani releases her Harajuku Lovers line of accessories; as the *L.A.M.B.* tour is beginning, Stefani learns that she is expecting a baby; on December 14 *Love. Angel. Music. Baby.* receives multiplatinum award status.

2006

Stefani and Rossdale welcome son Kingston James McGregor Rossdale on May 26; second solo CD, *The Sweet Escape,* is released on December 5.

2007

On June 25 *The Sweet Escape* reaches both gold and platinum award status.

2008

Stefani announces in January that she is expecting her second baby; she welcomes her second son, Zuma Nesta Rock Rossdale, on August 21.

For More Information

Books

Amy H. Blankstein, *Omnibus Press Presents the Story of Gwen Stefani*. London: Omnibus, 2005.

Kathleen Tracy, *Gwen Stefani*. Hockessin, DE: Mitchell Lane, 2007.

Internet Source

Mellowdee, *A Brief History of Ska*. www.youtube.com/watch?v=AesId12OKsY.

Web Sites

Backy Skank (http://users.bigpond.net.au/lvisser/skahistory.html). Web site of the Australian ska band Backy Skank. Includes a detailed history of the evolution of ska music.

Billboard (www.billboard.com). Web site of one of the most respected magazines in the music industry. Enter Gwen Stefani's name in the search box to access articles and reviews.

Gwen Stefani Official Web Site (www.gwenstefani.com). Official Web site of Gwen Stefani with news, tour information, photos, and links.

L, a L.A.M.B. Fragrance by Gwen Stefani (www.lambfragrance.com). Official Web site for Gwen Stefani's signature perfume.

L.A.M.B. Clothing Online Store (www.l-a-m-b.com). Official Web site for Gwen Stefani's clothing line.

No Doubt (www.nodoubt.com). Official Web site of the band No Doubt, featuring history and blogs.

No Doubt Scrapbook (www.nxdscrapbook.com/). This fan site archives articles about Stefani and No Doubt.

The Official Web Site of Jean Harlow (www.jeanharlow.com/index.php). Includes photos, biography, and filmography of the actress.

Discography

Albums with No Doubt

1992 *No Doubt*
1995 (March) *The Beacon Street Collection*
1995 (October) *Tragic Kingdom*
2000 *Return of Saturn*
2001 *Rock Steady*
2003 *No Doubt: The Singles, 1992–2003*

Solo Albums

2004 *Love. Angel. Music. Baby.*
2006 *The Sweet Escape*

DVDs

2004 *The Videos, 1992–2003*
2006 *Harajuku Lovers Live*
2006 *Live in the Tragic Kingdom*

CD/DVD Boxed Set

2004 *Boom Box*

Musical Adaptation CD

Rockabye Baby! Lullaby Renditions of No Doubt

Index

A

Andrews, Julie, 13, 24

The Aviator (film), 59–60

B

"Baggy Trousers" (song), 15, 30, 90

Ballard, Glen, 50

The Beacon Street Collection (album), 37, 38

Blender (magazine), 66

Bush (grunge band), 41

C

Cho, Margaret, 70

Cosmopolitan (magazine), 65, 90

D

DiCaprio, Leonardo, 59, *61*

"Don't Speak" (song), 44

Dumont, Tom, 23–24, 48, 82

E

Eve (rap singer), 51, 52

"Excuse Me Mr." (song), 45–46

F

Ferguson, Tony, 28, 38

"Fine By You" (song), 65

France, Kim, 44

G

Gonzalez, Gabriel, 18, 26

Grammy Awards, 57

H

Harajuku Girls (dancers), 68, *68–69*, 70

"Harajuku Girls" (song), 66, 68

Harajuku Lovers tour, *69*, 73, 75

Harajuku style, 66, 71, 72

Harlow, Jean, 60

"Hollaback Girl" (song), 68, 73

I

"I Throw My Toys Around" (song), 50

Interscope Records, 28, 30, 32, 34, 38

Iovine, Jimmy, 28, 65

J

"Just a Girl" (song), 6, 39, 41

K

Kanal, Tony, *14*, 24, *36*, 45, 82

joins No Doubt, 19–20

L

L.A.M.B. clothing, 62, 64, 71

Leal, Chris, 19

"Let Me Blow Ya Mind" (song), 51

Love. Angel. Music. Baby. (album), 66, 68

M

McMahon, Jerry, 19, 22

Meade, Alan, 18, 22
Meade, Tony, 18, 23
Music videos, 7, 31
  Don't Speak, 44–45
  Excuse Me Mr., 45–46
  Wind It Up, 13, 71, 77

N
No Doubt, 6–7
  birth of, 18–19
  first music video of, 31–32
  influences on, 24
  at the Roxy, 21
  signs first recording contract, 28
  in Warped Tour, 39
  wins Grammy Award, 57
No Doubt (album), 30–31, 48

P
Palmer, Paul, 38, 41
People (magazine), 11
Perry, Linda, 65

R
Recording industry Association of America (RIAA), 80
Return of Saturn (album), 50
"Rich Girl" (song), 68
Rock Steady (album), 51
Ross, Jonathan, 70
Rossdale, Gavin, 41, *42,* 51, 55, 78, *83*
Rossdale, Kingston James McGregor (son), *74,* 78, *79, 83*
  birth of, 75
Rossdale, Zuma Nesta Rock (son), 82
The Roxy (nightclub), 21

S
Scorsese, Martin, 59
Setzer, Brian, 50
Ska music, 15, 16
The Sound of Music (film), 13–14, 90
Spence, John, 18, 21
"Spiderwebs" (song), 42
Stefani, Dennis (father), 9, *10*
Stefani, Eric (brother), 9–10, *17,* 18, 21, 30, 32
  discovers ska music, 15–16
  leaves No Doubt, 34
Stefani, Gwen, *12, 67, 84, 87*
  becomes lead singer, 22
  birth of, 9
  break up with Tony Kanal, 35, 37
  with brother Eric, *17*
  charitable activities of, 80–82
  childhood of, 10–11, 13–14
  with DiCaprio, Leonardo, *61*
  fashion style of, 7–8, 85–87
  first solo album by, 65–66, 68
  Harajuku Girls and, 68, *68–69, 70*
  health problems of, 46
  with Kanal, Tony, *36*
  at L.A.M.B. fashion show, *63*
  launches fashion doll line, 77–78
  launches fragrance, 78–79
  launches L.A.M.B. clothing line, 62, 64
  with Leno, Jay, *58*

marries Gavin Rossdale, 54–55, 57
with members of No Doubt, *14, 33, 47, 81*
with parents, *10*
performance style of, 41, 42, 44
performing, *19, 20, 27, 29, 43, 69, 89*
on reporters' questions, 70–71
on *Return of Saturn,* 50
with Rossdale, Gavin, *49, 56, 83*
solo career of, 7
with son Kingston James, *79, 83*
on touring, 53
on touring while pregnant, 75
in Warped Tour, *40*
Stefani, Jill (sister), 9
Stefani, Patti (mother), 9, 10, *10,* 39
"Stick It in the Hole" (song), 16
The Sweet Escape (album), 76–77

T
Teen Vogue (magazine), 59
Tragic Kingdom (album), 6, 39, 46, 48, 57
achieves diamond award status, 80
sales of, 41, 51
"Trapped in a Box" (song), 31
Trauma Records, 38, 39

W
Warped Tour, 39, 40
Webb, Chris, 19, 23
"What You Waiting For?" (song), 66, 68
"Wind It Up" (song), 76
"Wonderful Life" (song), 76

Y
Young, Adrian, *14,* 51, 52, 82

Picture Credits

Cover photo: Michael Loccisano/FilmMagic/Getty Images
AP Images, 27, 62–63, 67, 68–69, 87
Michael Caulfield/WireImage/Getty Images, 88–89
Lee Celano/WireImage/Getty Images, 36
Lester Cohen/WireImage/Getty Images, 61
© Jody Cortes/Sygma/Corbis, 29
James Devaney/WireImage/Getty Images, 74, 84
© Trapper Frank/Corbis Sygma, 17
© Joe Giron/Corbis, 25
Jeff Vespa Archive/WireImage/Getty Images, 12
© Steve Jennings/Corbis, 33
Barry King/WireImage/Getty Images, 14, 20
Jean Baptiste Lacroix/WireImage/Getty Images, 83
Gary Livingston/Getty Images, 7
Kevin Mazur/WireImage/Getty Images, 10, 43
Frank Micelotta/Getty Images, 49
Tim Mosenfelder/Getty Images, 40
Jason Nevader/WireImage/Getty Images, 19
Thomas Rabsch/WireImage/Getty Images, 56
© Reuters/Corbis, 42
Ron Galella, Ltd./WireImage/Getty Images, 47
Matthew Simmons/Getty Images, 81
Marcel Thomas/FilmMagic/Getty Images, 79
Kevin Winter/ImageDirect/Getty Images, 58

About the Author

A native of Wisconsin, Anne K. Brown wanted to be a librarian when she was in second grade so she could spend time around all the books. A few lucky turns in her life landed her in a twenty-year career as an editor and writer—allowing her to spend lots of time around books. She collects vintage Nancy Drew books and repeatedly devours the writings of Roald Dahl.

Brown lives in a Milwaukee suburb with her husband, two daughters, and a black cat. This is her fifth published book.